PRAY FOR THE PEACE
OF JERUSALEM

PRAY FOR THE PEACE OF JERUSALEM

...Until Her Salvation
Shines Like a Blazing Torch
Isaiah 62:1

TOM HESS

First Printing   January 2000

Second Printing   January 2002

Third Printing   September 2005

ISBN: 965–7193–013–X

Published by:
Progressive Vision Publishing/
Jerusalem House of Prayer for All Nations
P.O. Box 31393
Jerusalem 91313
Israel
www.jhopfan.org
publishing@jhopfan.org

This book has been written, typeset and printed in Israel in agreement with Isaiah 2:3,

> **"The law will go out from Zion, and the word of the Lord from Jerusalem."**

Endorsements

Here a friend of the coming Bridegroom writes, making Him and His kingdom great. It reads like a central view of biblical prophecy. From all sides light falls on the hidden crossroads of human history in the Middle East. The deep mysteries of Jerusalem, the City of the Great King, are revealed.

At the same time this book is a torch that Tom Hess throws out to Jews and the nations worldwide, fanning the flame of obedience and passion for God's ways. Also, the 24-hour prayer movement that burns so strongly on his heart receives new inputs through this message.

**Geri Keller
Stiftung Schleife
Switzerland**

Tom Hess has unique insight into God's heart and purpose for the Middle East, Israel and Jerusalem and the relationship and responsibility of the Church to this glorious reality. Tom is a man of prayer and has paid the price to speak on the subjects in this book. I encourage all to read it who view themselves as intercessors with a heart to reach the whole world for the Messiah. Tom has done his homework theologically as well as spiritually. He is a blessed brother and this book will inspire and enlarge you as you receive its impartation and instruction.

**Mike Bickle
Director, International House of Prayer–Kansas City
Kansas City, Missouri, United States**

Tom Hess has been strategically placed on the Mount of Olives in these last days, where he carries the Lord's burden for Jerusalem, a topic about which there is much confusion. He loves and honors the Jewish and Arabic leaders of the Body of Messiah in Israel with equal fervor. May the Lord use this book to release fountains of prevailing, effective prayer for Jerusalem, Israel and the Arab Middle East at this critical hour.

**David Davis
Senior Pastor, Carmel Assembly
Haifa, Israel**

I keep a map of Jerusalem on the wall of my prayer closet as a reminder to pray daily for the peace of Jerusalem. Now, Tom Hess has provided this remarkable and thorough book providing powerful and practical patterns of understanding to significantly strengthen the impact of those prayers. This may well be one of the most important books ever written about Jerusalem, God's chosen people and the ultimate return of our Messiah, Jesus Christ.

Dr. Dick Eastman
International President, Every Home for Christ
Colorado Springs, Colorado, United States

In a time when the issue of Jerusalem is increasingly in the forefront of the world's attention, it is essential that our understanding of Jerusalem's calling and destiny will be more and more in accordance with God's plan for His city. As one who lives in Jerusalem, Tom has dedicated his life and ministry to the birthing and fulfillment of those aspects of Jerusalem's redemptive call that he describes in his new book *Pray for the Peace of Jerusalem...Until Her Salvation Shines Like a Blazing Torch*. Tom presents us with a large view of God's eternal purposes in His Son for Jerusalem and describes how in this city God sums up and fulfills the longings of His heart for the sons of Isaac and Ishmael, the Nations and the Church in these end-times and in all eternity.

Reuven Berger
Pastor, Congregation of the Messiah
Jerusalem, Israel

Tom Hess is one of the few people I know who, out of love for the Messiah Jesus, has entirely dedicated his life to Jerusalem, to the cause of the Jewish people, and reconciliation between Jews and Arabs.

This book will greatly help you understand the coherence of God's Kingdom with Jerusalem, Israel and the nations. But there is more to it. The book carries the reader away with a fervent love for the Messiah Jesus, whose splendor will dawn in His city, Jerusalem, through the restoration of Israel and through the reconciliation of all the children of Abraham, according to Isaiah 19. This will happen to the glory of the God of Israel and for the blessing of all the nations.

I highly recommend that you read this book, as it emerges from a sensitive and loving heart which is blessed with a deep understanding of the Scriptures.

Marcel Rebiai
Community of Reconciliation
Jerusalem, Israel

Tom Hess, who has spent more than 18 years in Jerusalem, has compiled a thought-provoking work in *Pray for the Peace of the Jerusalem*. He offers a comprehensive background of Jerusalem and shares God's revealed purposes for Israel and the Arab Middle East. Tom deserves commendations for his untiring efforts as a modern-day watchman and for his balanced and sincere book calling for believers to unite in faith to bring peace to Jerusalem.

This is a very timely book and well worth reading, especially in the light of the current situation in Jerusalem. I wholeheartedly recommend Tom's work to all readers who are genuinely concerned for the peace of Jerusalem.

Dr. Albert Isteero
Secretary Emeritus, Middle East Council of Churches
President Emeritus, Cairo Theological Seminary
Cairo, Egypt

"At that time his voice shook the earth, but now he has promised, 'Once more I will shake not only the earth but also the heavens.' ... Therefore, since we are receiving a kingdom that cannot be shaken, let us be thankful, and so worship God acceptably with reverence and awe, for our God is a consuming fire" (Hebrews 12:26,28-29).

As Israel and the entire Middle East are thrust further into the shaking of the end of this present age, intercessors all over the world earnestly seek an anchor of understanding and revelation into these difficult and exciting events. Consequently, much is being written and said today as many voices attempt to shed light and capture a sense of God's timing and purpose in the midst of trouble and trials.

Many of these attempts are speculative in nature, yet a few carry true revelatory encouragement and substance. Tom Hess' book, *Pray for the Peace of Jerusalem...Until Her Salvation Shines Like a Blazing Torch* is one such work. Deep in content, yet broad in spectrum, this work both searches the mysteries hidden in Jerusalem's earthly destiny and at the same time discovers the heavenly person of Jesus the Messiah, God's only begotten Son, the King of Jerusalem.

I wholeheartedly recommend both the book and the author. A good tree will produce good fruit, and I commit Tom's work to your prayer reading with the knowledge that you will be provoked, encouraged, and inspired to a higher, more devoted life of both prayer and worship.

Reuven Doron
Embrace Israel
Jerusalem, Israel

As we embrace the Lord's presence at the entrance of this new millennium, we would be wise to pay careful attention to those matters that are close and precious to God's heart. Without doubt, ancient Jerusalem will take center stage in the restoration of all things to come. This book is best read as a prophetic prayer to the Lord, Who is longing to bring forth His end-time purposes.

Dr. David Demian
Director, Watchmen for the Nations
Vancouver, Canada

The goal if this book is reconciliation and revival. Tom Hess' aim is always to exalt the Lord Jesus and to stir the saints of God to long and pray for biblical revival. For, "if God should create a hunger for the word of God," He will heal the people.

There are many books written on Jerusalem, but I believe this book is different, because it deals with real facts and events, which took place in the Holy Land. This book places at your fingertips practical, clear, and effective methods to reach and help people understand who Jesus the Messiah is. The book will help people to love God and other people so they do not end up in Hell.

Dr. Naim Khoury
Holy Land Baptist Mission
Bethlehem

Today, as Jerusalem rises to the cutting edge of prophetic fulfillment and the stage of history is being set for the end-time conflict and the coming of God's Kingdom, God is raising up a spiritual army of intercessors to stand in agreement with His purposes and plans. This book is a call for God's army to close the ranks of prayer and to equip the saints with knowledge and understanding for the task. I warmly recommend it.

Daniel Yahav
Peniel Fellowship
Tiberias, Israel

I like your book very much for the insight that it provides on the controversial subject of Jerusalem. What you have to say about the importance of Jerusalem, the most important city in the entire world, is very interesting.

I congratulate you for this good work which I hope every Jewish and Arab pastor will read for it is biblically based and well balanced.

Afeef Halasah
Pastor, Nazarene Church
A Moabite of Amman, Jordan

I fully recommend *Pray for the Peace of Jerusalem* as a very helpful book. God has given Tom Hess the vision and the burden for peace and reconciliation for Jerusalem and the nation of Israel. His effort to this effect has in a tremendous way, changed the views and attitudes of people around the world. *Pray for the Peace of Jerusalem* will help readers understand more about the burden and will enhance fulfillment of the vision.

> **Mered Lemma**
> **Pastor, Addis Ababa Full Gospel Believers' Church**
> **Addis Ababa, Ethiopia**

The timing for a volume on *Pray for the Peace of Jerusalem* could not have been better. Tom Hess' unique perspective from the Mount of Olives and prophetic insights into the crucial issues underlying the current escalation in the battle over Jerusalem, make this book essential reading for all of us who watch and pray for Messiah's return to the City of Peace.

> **David Lazarus**
> **Pastor, Beit Avinu Congregation**
> **Tel Aviv/Jaffa, Israel**

Rich in historical content, solid in biblical truth, and timely in prophetic insight, *Pray for the Peace of Jerusalem* reveals the profound significance of events we see unfolding daily in the Middle East in our newspapers and on our television screens. Tom clearly outlines God's eternal plan for His Holy City, Jerusalem. You will not only benefit from the wealth of spiritual understanding offered in this volume, but you will come away with pragmatic ways to partner with God in His plans for this city and people, both through prayer and practical responses.

> **Jane Hansen**
> **Aglow International**
> **Edmonds, Washington, United States**

This landmark book, *Pray for the Peace of Jerusalem*, gives the world one of the most excellent, well researched and comprehensive studies of this critical subject. His factual, yet profoundly spiritual approach gives the most scholarly, as well as the new student of the Bible, an appreciation of this subject matter. I highly recommend this work to every serious student of the Bible and prophecy. It will ignite your love for the God of Israel and rekindle your respect and understanding of the City of Messiah.

> **Dr. Myles Munroe**
> **Bahamas Faith Ministries**
> **Nassau, Bahamas**

Pray for the Peace of Jerusalem emerged in a time when the Holy Spirit is calling the Body of Christ worldwide to the watchman ministry. As an apostle and watchman in Jerusalem, Tom Hess gives the most exhaustive treatment that I know of, concerning the relationship between the salvation of Jerusalem and the salvation of the nations. Jerusalem is the main gate to the gates of the nations.

This book is a powerful tool the Holy Spirit has put in the hands of intercessors and watchmen to prepare the Church for the coming harvest and to prepare the way for the second advent of Messiah.

Reverend Dr. Niko Njotorahardjo
Senior Pastor, GBI Bethany Church
Jakarta, Indonesia

There is probably no harder scripture to apply concerning Israel as this command of the Lord. It is even harder in these last days of turmoil, confusing political sentiments and end-time prophetic fulfillment. Therefore Tom Hess' book is more than timely to guide the Church worldwide on how to pray for the peace of Jerusalem. It provides the clarity and light that has been missing. I have had the opportunity to work with Tom Hess among Jewish and Arab congregations in Israel and I know that what he shares in this book has been taught to him by God through experience.

This book is a must for all Christians.

Pastor John Mulinde
World Trumpet Mission & Watchman Intercessors Network
Kampala, Uganda

To pray for the peace of Jerusalem means you must work for the peace of Jerusalem. To work for the peace of Jerusalem means you have to love the people of Jerusalem—both Jew and Arab. To seek the true peace of Jerusalem means you must understand God's prophetic calling on this city and land that is called holy. Tom Hess lives in this complex reality. *Pray for the Peace of Jerusalem* is the most profound book I have ever read on this subject. To read it is a must for all who love this desperate, broken and holy city.

Canon Andrew White
Director of the International Centre for Reconciliation &
The Archbishop of Canterbuty's Special Representative to
the Middle East Peace Process

Contents

Acknowledgments

This book, *Pray for the Peace of Jerusalem...Until Her Salvation Shines Like a Blazing Torch,* has been written from the trenches of the battle for Jerusalem, so to speak.

The book you have in your hands is the result of living in Jerusalem (both East and West Jerusalem), having founded and served as the pastor of Messianic Community of Reconciliation and International Director of Jerusalem House of Prayer for All Nations on the Mount of Olives, since its establishment in 1987. Jerusalem House of Prayer for All Nations has coordinated 50 All Jerusalem, All Israel and All Middle East, All 10/40 Window and All Nations Convocations during this time. I have led prayer walks and have spoken throughout Israel and most of the Arab nations for 18 years. As the Messianic Community of Reconciliation–Jerusalem House of Prayer for All Nations have worshiped, watched, worked and prayed through the whole *intifada* from 1987 through the Gulf War in 1991, and the second *intifada* that began in the year 2000. I am especially indebted to those fellow laborers who have walked together with me on the journey of seeing the first-fruits of Egypt, Israel and Assyria becoming a blessing in the midst of the earth through many shakings over these years. The shakings will become much more severe before this promise is fulfilled to completion.

My thanks go to these Jewish and Arab heroes of the faith, many of whom have sacrificed the ease and comfort of living in Western nations and are laying down their lives as prayers for the peace of Jerusalem: Reuven Berger, Bassam Adranley, Marcel Rebiai, Nizar Shaheen (all from Jerusalem), Daniel Yahav (Tiberias), David Davis (Haifa), Avner Boskey (Be'er Sheva), David Lazarus and Avi Mizrachi (Tel Aviv), Naim Khoury (Bethlehem), Afeef Halasah (Jordan), Dr. Albert Isteero (Egypt), Dr. David Demian (an Egyptian living in Canada), John Mulinde (Uganda), to name a few, but there are also many others. Many of these friends have graciously endorsed this book.

Their focus have been more on the promises than on the problems. Consequently, they are the first-fruits of Isaiah 19:23-25 and also the first-fruits of many coming to faith in Messiah in the midst of great shakings. They are Joshuas and Calebs on God's dream team from Egypt, Israel and Assyria, who are dreaming with Abraham, Moses, Joshua, Isaiah, David and Jesus about the restoration of the peace of Jerusalem. While they see the giants in the land, they see the Lord and His promises as greater than the giants. They say this is a good land flowing with milk and honey and have chosen to work and pray for her peace because they have seen that they are more than able to possess the land.

I have written out of the context of the challenges of ministering to the King of Jerusalem and His people, the Jews and Arabs, waiting upon and trying to listen to the Father's heart for Jerusalem over the years. I have written *Pray for the Peace of Jerusalem* after traveling in over 140 nations and being asked many times what it means to pray for the peace of Jerusalem. I realized then that no in-depth book has ever been written to address this often asked question.

I hope that as you read this book you will also become Joshuas and Calebs and join God's dream team, the World Wide Watch for Jerusalem, watching, worshiping and praying for the peace of Jerusalem.

I also want to thank Johan de Meyer for assisting in editing and designing this book and Liaza Valster for making the banner that appears on the cover. Both are from South Africa.

I hope *Pray for the Peace of Jerusalem* will help both Jews and Gentiles to better understand the multi-faceted dimensions of the meaning of Jerusalem and the struggle for Jerusalem we are facing, and lead you to more effectively pray and work for her peace. It is all about Messiah whose salvation will soon shine upon Jerusalem like a blazing torch.

Shalom to Jerusalem with her King,

Tom Hess
Jerusalem and Caesarea, Israel
September 2005

Chapter 1

Pray for the Peace of Jerusalem Until Her Salvation Shines Like a Blazing Torch

Pray for the Peace of Jerusalem— All Those Who Love Her Shall Prosper (Be Secure)

"But you have come to Mount Zion, the heavenly Jerusalem, the city of the living God. You have come to thousands upon thousands of angels in joyful assembly, to the church of the firstborn, whose names are written in heaven. You have come to God, the judge of all men, to the spirits of righteous men made perfect, to Jesus the mediator of a new covenant, and to the sprinkled blood that speaks a better word than the blood of Abel" (Hebrews 12:22-24).

"But the Jerusalem that is above is free and she is our mother" (Galatians 4:26).

"I rejoiced with those who said to me, 'Let us go to the House of the LORD.'"

"Our feet are standing in your gates, O Jerusalem. Jerusalem is built like a city that is closely compacted together. That is where the tribes go up, the tribes of the LORD, to praise the name of the LORD according to the statute given to Israel. There the thrones for judgment stand, the thrones of the house of David.

"Pray for the peace of Jerusalem: 'May those who love you be secure. May there be peace within your walls and security in your citadels.' For the sake of my brothers and friends, I will say, 'Peace be within you.' For the sake of the house of the LORD our God, I will seek your prosperity" (Psalm 122).

This book is about Jerusalem, from the Garden of Eden to the eternal city, the new Jerusalem, coming down from heaven; about the heavenly and earthly Jerusalem, how they were divided at the fall of man and how they will be united forever in Messiah when He comes down from heaven. The shepherds said at Bethlehem: "Glory to God in the Highest and peace on earth and good will towards men!" John 1:14 says that the Word—from heaven—became flesh on earth and tabernacled among us.

In Messiah's triumphant entry on Palm Sunday, four proclamations were made. Two proclamations were made regarding heaven, "Hosanna in the Highest" and "Glory to the Highest," and two regarding the earth, "Hosanna to the Son of David" and "Hosanna to the King of Israel." The purpose of Messiah is the restoration of the heavenly Jerusalem on earth, in fulfillment of Jesus' prayer: "Let Thy Kingdom come on earth as it is in heaven." Praying for the peace of Jerusalem means heavenly and earthly Jerusalem are being united as one in Messiah Yeshua.

Jerusalem means **the peace** (*Salem*, who is Messiah) that **comes down** (*Jeru*) **from heaven** and **is laid** as a foundation cornerstone in this city, and then His Word is **sent out** (*Jeru*) as teaching to the ends of the world. In these last days of shakings and salvation, pray that God will hasten and fulfill His full purpose, meaning and destiny for Jerusalem.

Jerusalem Consists of Two Hebrew Words—*Jeru* and *Salem*

Albert Einstein, a Jew who was declared "The Man of the 20th Century" by *Time Magazine*, was a genius. Dr. Einstein made a very profound statement when he said, "I want to know God's thoughts, the rest are details." This statement has great ramifications in regard to the peace of Jerusalem. In Isaiah 55:8-9, God says that His thoughts are higher than our thoughts, even as the heavens are higher than the earth. In Isaiah 2:3, the nations say, "Come let us go up to the mountain of the Lord, to the house of the God of Jacob, for He will teach (*Jeru*) us his ways so we will walk in His paths. The law (*Jeru*) will go out (*Jeru*) from Zion and the Word of the Lord from Jerusalem." God's thoughts and purpose is to restore, bring down (*Jeru*) peace/*shalom* to earth as it is in heaven.

Daniel Yahav, a Jewish *sabra* born in Jaffa, Israel, now residing in Tiberias, once shared with me a meaning of Jerusalem that I had not heard before. Jerusalem consists of two words *Jeru* and *Salem*. The Hebrew word *Jeru* means to lay down a foundation or to cast down from above (Job 38: 6; Gen. 31:51). Abraham laying down stones and building altars and laying down Isaac, could be interpreted as a picture of God laying down out of Zion Yeshua His Son, as the chief cornerstone, sure foundations (Isa. 28: 16). (See also the next section.) In II Samuel 11:20 and II Chronicles 35: 23, *Jeru* means that God's peace will not only be laid down as a foundation from heaven above where God is, but *Jeru* also means to teach the law, to shoot out horizontally. If we seek God, not only will He teach us His ways of peace from heaven above, but we will also walk in His paths of peace. The law will *Jeru* (go out—shot/taught) from Zion (on earth) and the word of the Lord from Jerusalem. Only when this happens in fullness, will swords be turned into plowshares and spears into pruning hooks and they will train for war no more.

Jeru Means Coming, Shooting Out, and Laying Down

1. On Moriah (teaches), God provides a Ram and comes down (*Jeru*).

2. When the Law was given to Moses, it came down (*Jeru*) from Heaven.

3. Jesus as the Chief Rabbi-Teacher and apostle comes down as the Lamb of God, as the ultimate fulfillment of Isaac offered as a sacrifice (Gal. 1).

4. Jesus comes down in the second coming.

5. A man can receive nothing unless it comes down from heaven. We will only receive real *shalom* in Jerusalem on earth when it is *Jeru*—

laid down from heaven. "See I lay a stone in Zion, a tested stone, a precious cornerstone for a sure foundation; the one who trusts will never be dismayed" (Isa. 28:16). We need to pray with King David as he did in Psalm 14:7, "Oh, that the salvation of Israel would come out (*Jeru*) of Zion! When the Lord restores the fortunes of his people, let Jacob rejoice and Israel be glad!"

6.   · The Gospel of peace shoots out to the ends of the earth.

7.   The law of peace will go forth to all nations, shooting out in the millennium.

8.   The new Jerusalem comes down (*Jeru*) from heaven as a bride prepared for her bridegroom.

Salem Means King of Righteousness and King of Peace (Heb. 7:1-2)

Salem, which means an inheritance of peace, will only come to Israel when they have God as their inheritance. Peace will only come to Jerusalem when the Jews receive their inheritance, their Messiah, who is the King of Righteousness, the King of Peace. Their peace is all about and will only be found in Messiah, who is the only way to peace and is the Prince of Peace and the King of Peace. Without the King of Peace, all the negotiations in the world will be fruitless. With the true King of Peace, true peace will be restored immediately. Many Jews and Gentiles are looking for Messiah to emerge from out of the earth to bring world unity and peace. I Thessalonians says: "This peace will be a false peace. People will be crying: Peace, peace, then will come destruction." The reason we see no light at the end of the tunnel in the Middle East peace process is because we are looking for peace from man's humanistic planning instead of knowing that God's thoughts and ways of peace are much higher than ours. If Jews, Arabs and believers from the nations follow these words of Einstein and seek God's thoughts on *shalom*/peace instead of man's, we will find *shalom* in our lives and in Jerusalem and the other details can be worked out. Otherwise we will continue in deception, despair, dissolution, dead ends and destruction. This book is an attempt to point you toward God's thoughts about the *shalom* (peace) of Jerusalem. If we are going to, for the sake of the House of the Lord our God, seek Jerusalem's prosperity as stated in Psalm 122:9, Jerusalem will only really prosper when she receives her Messiah; until then she will not have real prosperity, only problems. We must seek the Lord and His perfect thoughts, ways and paths of peace and prosperity and not continue following man's futile thoughts, plans and ways.

Some people are living primarily for financial prosperity or security as they pray for the peace of Jerusalem and this could be part of the blessing. But I have also seen people get attacked financially when they get involved with Jerusalem. From Jesus' perspective, prosperity is primarily spiritual. When we seek, pray and work for the peace of Jerusalem, for God's heart and with His love, we are laying up treasures in heaven where moth and rust do not destroy and where thieves cannot rob or steal. For where your treasure is, there your heart will be also. If we truly love the King of Jerusalem and have His heart for Jews, Arabs and people from all nations and are praying and working for the peace of Jerusalem, we will surely be laying up treasures in heaven, be secure and prosper spiritually as He promised! The Church in the first century in Jerusalem desired and saw their needs met in the earthly Jerusalem even as if they were in heaven. May God help us to do the same today.

To love Jerusalem means first and foremost to love the King and Messiah of Jerusalem, because Jerusalem is all about Him. Unless we love and know Him properly, we will never be able to have His heart and compassion for the people of His city and love her properly as the believers did in the first century.

Many Christian tourists come to spend their time seeing the Jerusalem stones, the Western Wall or church buildings, visiting tourist sites, jewelry or gift shops, archeological digs or planting trees. All these things are nice and good, but have no or little connection with what God loves about Jerusalem. If we are living in, visiting or praying for this great city from afar, we need to love what God loves about her.

Ask God to give you the fullness of love for Him as her King and then He will give you His love, compassion and heart for His city and people.

"O Jerusalem, Jerusalem, you who kill the prophets and stone those sent to you, how often I have longed to gather your children together, as a hen gathers her chicks under her wings, but you were not willing. Look, your house is left to you desolate. For I tell you, you will not see me again until you say, 'Blessed is he who comes in the name of the Lord'" (Matthew 23:37-39).

"Jesus went through all the towns and villages, teaching in their synagogues, preaching the good news of the kingdom and healing every disease and sickness. When he saw the crowds, he had compassion on them, because they were harassed and helpless like sheep without a shepherd. Then he said to his disciples, 'The harvest is plentiful but the workers are few. Ask the Lord of the harvest, therefore, to send out workers into his harvest field'" (Matthew 9:35-38).

If we love Jerusalem (the Jewish and Arab people), we will greatly prosper. We are called to love what God loves about Jerusalem. He loves the peoples of Jerusalem—Jews, Arabs and others. This is what He shed His blood for and where He shed it. He also loves the city because it will be the place for the soles of His feet forever. This is where the new Jerusalem will be, and where His bride will be with Him forever.

He who loves Jerusalem will prosper eternally and be secure in her King forever, as a part of the new Jerusalem.

Pray for the Peace of Jerusalem ... Until Her Salvation Shines Like a Blazing Torch has been written to:

1. Encourage all of us as sons and daughters of Father God to grow and fall more and more in love with the King of Jerusalem;

2. Emphasize that Jerusalem's peace is coming from above and only found by and will only come to the Jews, Arabs and those from the nations who know and follow Jesus as the Bridegroom/King/Warrior/Peacemaker/Messiah;

3. Show how all blood sacrifice by God's people led to the ultimate fulfilment in the shedding of the blood of Messiah, the Prince of Peace, once and for all as the ultimate sacrifice in Jerusalem;

4. Trace Jerusalem's development and highlight significant dates throughout its history from before father Abraham to Messiah's coming;

5. Reveal how Bible history flows from two trees in Genesis to one tree in Revelation; how the natural branches (Jews) and wild branches (Gentiles) are both grafted into the olive tree and how the leaves of this tree, representing the Tree of Life, are for the healing of the nations;

6. Show the significance of Abraham as the father of us all and how seeing things with the same eyes and vision he had, helps us see things and then build not temporal but eternal foundations;

7. Explain what the ten stones are and to show how praying and working for their removal will prepare the way for ultimate peace coming to Jerusalem in Messiah's coming as King;

8. Help people pray that God's work as revealed in Zechariah 12-14, which tells of 16 things God will do in the last days in Jerusalem, will be hastened to bring and prepare the way for God's ultimate peace to come to Jerusalem;

9. Encourage people to pray for understanding of how God's redemptive purpose for the Church in our nations is connected with His redemptive purpose for Israel as we are both called together to be a light to the nations (Isa. 42:6; Matt. 5:14); and

10. Understand how to worship, pray and work for the peace of Jerusalem, that the Lord Himself will be a wall of fire around her and her glory within. We need to pray that Jerusalem will be shielded by her King, even as she is encircled with prayer and worship from watches and revivals around the earth. May He be manifest as her glory within, culminating in His ultimate coming as King of Jerusalem when the fullness of her glory will be revealed as a blazing torch.

This book shows how earth and the heavenly Jerusalem were divided at the Fall of man in the Garden of Eden and how father Abraham started the restoration process. This process continued under David, Solomon, especially through Jesus' first coming, His second soon coming down (*Jeru*) from heaven making her salvation shine like a blazing torch, and the new Jerusalem coming down from heaven. The seven candlestick *menorah* continually burns in heaven. Israel's national symbol is also a *menorah* and as Israel is called to be a light to the nations, so the Church is called to be the light of the world. God is lighting 24-hour Watches all over the earth, as in heaven, with continual fires burning on the altars. Yet, in the new Jerusalem there will be no *menorah* (lamp) as the Lamb, our Salvation, is the only light shining through eternity as a blazing torch (see the maps and pictures in chronological order at the back of the book). As it is commonly said, "A picture is worth a thousand words."

Pray with us for the peace of Jerusalem until her salvation shines like a blazing torch!

Chapter 2

The Great King of Jerusalem— It's All About Messiah

Wa hen Jesus appeared to John in Revelation 1, His appearance was like a blazing torch, His eyes were like blazing fire, His feet were like bronze glowing in a furnace, and His face was like the sun shining in all its brilliance. Hebrews 12 says God will shake everything that can be shaken. Let us be thankful and so worship God, for our God is a consuming fire. The days until Messiah comes will be days of great shakings and great salvation, as God manifests Himself in increasing ways as a consuming fire, a blazing torch, a wall of fire around Jerusalem and her glory within.

Jerusalem will be the future habitation of the Great King, who is also a bridegroom, a friend and Messiah. He is altogether lovely and He is waiting for His people to prepare themselves as a bride does for her bridegroom. There is a place of intimacy with this Great King that is yet to be fully discovered. It is a restoration of the close communion that existed in the Garden of Eden before the Fall. Even as heaven and earth were one before the Fall, so again as Ephesians 1:10 says, all things in heaven and on earth will be united in Messiah.

The Shulamite woman speaks to the daughters of Jerusalem about the Great King:

> "My lover is radiant and ruddy, outstanding among ten thousand. His head is purest gold; his hair is wavy and black as a raven. His eyes are like doves by the water streams, washed in milk, mounted like jewels. His cheeks are like beds of spice yielding perfume. His lips are like lilies dripping with myrrh. His arms are rods of gold set with chrysolite. His body is like

polished ivory decorated with sapphires. His legs are pillars of marble set on bases of pure gold. His appearance is like Lebanon, choice as its cedars. His mouth is sweetness itself; he is altogether lovely. This is my lover, this is my friend, O daughters of Jerusalem" (Song of Songs 5:10-16).

The primary reason for Jerusalem's importance in the physical and spiritual realities of our world is that it belongs to the Great King, who longs to be reunited with his bride for eternity. The city is called great, only because of the Great King who will inhabit it eternally as the Bridegroom-Lamb-Lion-King.

This is the reason for writing this book. As will be explained later, every believer on the planet has the responsibility primarily to prepare himself to meet the Great King when He comes and secondarily, to pray for the peace of Jerusalem that the city may be prepared as the Great King's eternal habitation.

If we understand God's heart for this city and its people, we will respond to His call. The King is calling His watchmen to stand with Him for the place where His feet will dwell for eternity.

"I have posted watchmen on your walls, O Jerusalem; they will never be silent day or night. You who call on the LORD, give yourselves no rest, and give him no rest till he establishes Jerusalem and makes her the praise of the earth" (Isaiah 62:6-7).

Psalm 48:1-2 says,

"Great is the Lord and most worthy of praise, in the city of our God, his holy mountain. It is beautiful in its loftiness, the joy of the whole earth. Like the utmost heights of Zaphon is Mount Zion, the city of the Great King."

The Great King is awesome in His majesty and greatness. He is the Great King who came to earth, humbled Himself and became obedient to the point of death and died as the ultimate sacrifice for the sins of humanity, thereby accomplishing what Isaac's death could not have. Only because of

His splendor is Mount Zion called great, because He endured the cross; only because of His sweet presence will this city become the joy of the whole earth.

> "There is a river whose streams make glad the city of God, the holy place where the Most High dwells. God is within her, she will not fall; God will help her at break of day. Nations are in uproar, kingdoms fall; he lifts his voice, the earth melts.
>
> The Lord Almighty is with us; the God of Jacob is our fortress. Come and see the works of the Lord, the desolations he has brought on the earth. He makes wars cease to the ends of the earth; he breaks the bow and shatters the spear, he burns the shields with fire.
>
> 'Be still, and know that I am God; I will be exalted among the nations, I will be exalted in the earth.'
>
> The Lord Almighty is with us; the God of Jacob is our fortress" (Psalm 46:4-11).

The river and streams flowing from God's throne (Eden/Paradise) make glad the city of God, the holy place where the Most High dwells. This is the significance of Jerusalem. It is the holy place where the Most High dwells, and it is His streams that make the city glad. As will be explained later, it is possibly the place where He walked with Adam in the Garden of Eden. It is the place father Abraham is still looking for—a place with foundations whose builder and founder is God (Hebrews 11:10). It is the Holy City of God. It is the place where God dwelt when His *shekhina* glory filled the Temple of Solomon and where the veil of the Temple was rent when Yeshua died. It is where Yeshua rose again, breathed on His disciples and said, "*Shalom* [peace] be with you! ... Receive the Holy Spirit" (John 20:21-22). He prepared the first-fruit of the spiritual temple of living stones (the new Jerusalem) coming down from heaven.

In Psalm 132:14, He said, "**this is my** [God's] **resting place for ever and ever; here will I sit enthroned, for I have desired it.**" He has destined it for His habitation. Ezekiel says it is the place of the soles of His feet forever:

"I heard someone speaking to me from inside the temple. He said: 'Son of man, this is the place of my throne and the place for the soles of my feet. This is where I will live among the Israelites forever. The house of Israel will never again defile my holy name'" (Ezekiel 43:6-7).

Yet we tend to look at Jerusalem from our own perspective, wondering whether it will ever be a Holy City because of all its problems. It is true that we will see very difficult times in the coming years before Messiah returns, as Satan takes his last stand. All nations will come against Jerusalem:

"I will gather all the nations to Jerusalem to fight against it; the city will be captured, the houses ransacked, and the women raped. Half of the city will go into exile, but the rest of the people will not be taken from the city" (Zechariah 14:2).

Although we tend to panic, fear and get stressed out, from God's perspective it is finished! He has already disarmed the devil and evil powers through the cross and rendered them powerless. He is standing for His city right now and is calling us to stand with Him—to be watchmen with Him for Jerusalem.

"On that day, when all the nations of the earth are gathered against her, I will make Jerusalem an immovable rock for all nations. All who try to move it will injure themselves" (Zechariah 12:3).

In 1990, the Lord said to me, "I want you to stand with Me for Jerusalem. Many will leave in the most afflicted days but I am calling you to stand." As believers today, we should be a first-fruit community that is like a colony of heaven in Jerusalem, representing the Great King in His city and preparing the way for His total and complete takeover. For the Lord says, "I am making everything new" (Revelation 21:5). We need to faithfully stand with Him until it is fully accomplished.

Today the Lord says we are to put on the whole armor of God that we may be able to stand. Stand your ground. Having done everything, still stand as He stood in Jerusalem. Today, the Lord says to Satan, "**The Lord** rebuke you, Satan. **The Lord, who has chosen Jerusalem, rebuke you!"** **(Zechariah 3:2).** The angel Michael is about to blow the great shofar in heaven, signalling the day when the Father will release the Great King to take up His throne in Jerusalem.

The Great King will annihilate the enemy and all the nations—who are like a drop in the bucket—that oppose His plan to take up His throne in Jerusalem forever. He will cast out and bind Satan and take over Jerusalem forever and make her new and reign as her Great King forever. Then the prophetic scriptures will be fulfilled.

In relation to eternity, the length of time that Jerusalem will not totally be a holy city (because the King of the city is not dwelling there in fullness) is merely a few days. A day of eternity is more than a thousand years. From God's perspective all the rulers of history—the Romans, Crusaders, Muslims and Turks, the British and all others—had Jerusalem for a few days of eternity. But the God of Israel is ready to overthrow all these negative forces and to release His Son. The Messiah will come from heaven and then the heavenly Jerusalem will manifest on earth as in heaven. Before that time, Islam, the Babylonian peace plan, the New Age Movement, Freemasonry, Kaballah, all false religions and false messiahs and cults will be finished forever. God says,

> **"On that day a fountain will be opened to the house of David and the inhabitants of Jerusalem, to cleanse them from sin and impurity. On that day I will banish the names of the idols from the land, and they will be remembered no more," declares the Lord Almighty. "I will remove both the prophets and the spirit of impurity from the land" (Zechariah 13:1-2).**

God says to the people of Jerusalem, as He has said to many biblical heroes of faith in the past, "Be still and know that I am God. Stand still and see the salvation of God. I will fight for you, only be still!" We are to help prepare the house for battle but the victory for Jerusalem already belongs to the Great King. Jerusalem will eventually be the completely realized Holy City of God throughout eternity, except for this very short period of time when God is allowing the enemy to finish playing out his hand!

Once everything has been made new, the whole world will see the Great King as the only great and significant thing about Jerusalem. His name will be the only name. Jerusalem is and will be all and only about Him! Then the Lord God will reign as the Great King of Jerusalem forever and He will be the holy Host for all of her inhabitants forever. Hallelujah!

> "If I forget you, O Jerusalem, may my right hand forget its skill, may my tongue cling to the roof of my mouth if I do not remember you, if I do not consider Jerusalem my highest joy" (Psalm 137:5-6).

King David said if he did not remember Jerusalem and consider Jerusalem his highest joy, that his right hand should forget its skill and his tongue cling to the roof of his mouth. Why did he say this? Because as Isaiah says,

> "No longer will they call you Deserted, or name your land Desolate. But you will be called Hephzibah, and your land Beulah; for the LORD will take delight in you, and your land will be married. As a young man marries a maiden, so will your sons marry you; as a bridegroom rejoices over his bride, so will your God rejoice over you. I have posted watchmen on your walls, O Jerusalem; they will never be silent day or night. You who call on the LORD, give yourselves no rest, and give Him no rest till he establishes Jerusalem and makes her the praise of the earth" (Isaiah 62:4-7).

Not only is the bride married to the bridegroom, the King of Jerusalem, but the city and land of Jerusalem are to be married to the Lord. He is about to take it back as His capital **Jerusalem**, like the Garden of Eden on earth before the Fall, as a blessing in the midst of the earth. It is meant to be the capital of the Jews only because it belongs to Him and He is the King of the Jews. Without Him on His throne in His city, there will be no *shalom* (peace). Jerusalem will never fully be the capital of the Jews until they recognize their King, their Cornerstone, welcome Him home and give Him His rightful place in the city! He will also be the King of the Arabs and all nations. When He returns, Jerusalem will be our highest joy for all eternity because it will be the dwelling place of our Great King who is our highest joy. David said again in Psalm 16:11, **"You will fill me with joy in your presence, eternal pleasures are at your right hand."**

Abraham understood this and went looking for a city that has foundations, whose builder and maker is God—for the new Jerusalem coming down from heaven. The Lord loves the gates of Zion even more than all the dwellings of Jacob:

> **"He has set his foundation on the holy mountain; the LORD loves the gates of Zion even more than all the dwellings of Jacob. Glorious things are said of you, O city of God" (Psalm 87:1-3).**

If Jerusalem is great only because of her Great King, it means that we can only understand the city if we know the Great King. Only through our relationship with the King can we ever hope to understand why this city is of any importance at all. If it is such a point of contention, why not abandon it and start over somewhere else? Because the Great King has His eyes on this place. To reject Jerusalem would be like rejecting the King and His purposes.

The more we understand the nature and character of God, the more we will understand that God's heart is broken over Jerusalem and Jerusalem's rejection of Him as her Great King. He came to Jerusalem to show us how to live and to die for our sins that we may live but the Great King, the last Adam, was rejected as her king. He wept over Jerusalem:

> **"O Jerusalem, Jerusalem, you who kill the prophets and stone those sent to you, how often I have longed to gather your children together, as a hen gathers her chicks under her wings, but you were not willing! Look, your house is left to you desolate. I tell you, you will not see me again until you say, 'Blessed is he who comes in the name of the LORD'" (Luke 13:34-35).**

> **"As he approached Jerusalem and saw the city, he wept over it and said, 'If you, even you, had only known on this day what would bring you peace—but now it is hidden from your eyes. The days will come upon you when your enemies will build an embankment against you and encircle you and hem you in on every side. They will dash you to the ground, you and**

the children within your walls. They will not leave one stone on another, because you did not recognize the time of God's coming to you'" (Luke 19:41-44).

The King of the Jews and of Jerusalem came to earth for Jerusalem's sake, died and rose again. This all began in the Garden of Eden when Adam and Eve rejected life, chose death and paradise fell. Heaven and earth were separated, and God destroyed the world by the flood.

Then God raised up Abraham to see Jerusalem with God's vision, to bring the city back to God, as he met Melchizedek (Jesus), the King of Jerusalem. They broke bread and drank wine together. Abraham came to Jerusalem, built an altar and offered his son Isaac to God as a foreshadowing of the redemption of Jerusalem through Jesus, the ultimate Redeemer. He saw Jesus' day, even the new Jerusalem, the city which had foundations, whose builder and maker is God. The Jews failed Him, although He came to die for their sins. He was for the most part rejected as her King.

King David also had a vision of Jerusalem and after 24-hour worship was established in Jerusalem, God prepared the way for her natural borders to span from the Nile to the Euphrates. God says,

"I will record Rahab and Babylon among those who acknowledge me—Philistia too, and Tyre, along with Cush—and will say, 'This one was born in Zion'" (Psalm 87:4).

God is the Great King of Jerusalem and He watches over her and prays for her peace. He is waiting for watchmen to arise to join Him in intimacy and intercession. God so loved the world that He sent Messiah to die in Jerusalem as the King of the Jews for her peace and the peace of all nations. He is God because of who He is. God is the Great King of Jerusalem. His nature and character was, is and will be manifest in this city through the Messiah King.

"My heart is stirred by a noble writer as I recite my verses for the king, my tongue is the pen of a skillful writer. You are the most excellent of men and your lips have been anointed with grace, since God has blessed you forever. Gird your sword upon your side, O mighty one; clothe yourself with splendor and majesty.

In your majesty ride forth victoriously in behalf of truth, humility and righteousness; let your right hand display awesome deeds. Let your sharp arrows pierce the hearts of the king's enemies; let the nations fall beneath your feet.

Your throne, O God, will last forever and ever; a scepter of justice will be the scepter of your kingdom. You love righteousness and hate wickedness; therefore God, your God, has set you above your companions by anointing you with the oil of joy. All your robes are fragrant with myrrh and aloes and cassia; from palaces adorned with ivory the music of the strings makes you glad. Daughters of kings are among your honored women; at your right hand is the royal bride in gold of Ophir.

Listen, O daughter, consider and give ear; Forget your people and your father's house. The king is enthralled by your beauty; honor him, for he is your lord. The Daughter of Tyre will come with a gift, men of wealth will seek your favor. All glorious is the princess within her chamber; her gown is interwoven with gold. In embroidered garments she is led to the king; her virgin companions follow her and are brought to you. They are led in with joy and gladness; they enter the palace of the king. Your sons will take the place of your fathers; you will make them princes throughout the land. I will perpetuate your memory through all generations; therefore the nations will praise you for ever and ever" (Psalm 45).

The Great and Holy One of Israel, who is without sin and inhabits eternity will inhabit Jerusalem forever as her Great King. The Lord's nature and character have been revealed in the way that He has dealt with Jerusalem. His first and second coming will pave the way for the new Jerusalem to descend to earth. Even in the times of her desolation, the prophets have emphasized that these times are set and appointed. God remains in control of His Holy City. The way He has dealt with it reveals His nature and character in multi-faceted ways.

God Is Love

The Lord God Almighty loves us with an everlasting love. His loving kindness is better than life, and He has engraved us on the palm of His hand.

The purpose for God creating man in His own image and likeness was to have someone with whom to share His infinite love—someone who could eternally experience the depth, height, breadth and width of His love, which surpasses all knowledge and understanding.

Because man rejected His love and His desire to share His love with man, a great division came about between heaven and earth. But God did not give up in His passion and desire to have a people, a bride with whom He could share the unfathomable riches of His love. He so loved the world that He sent His Son to Jerusalem to be offered up as the ultimate love sacrifice for the sins of the world in the same place where Abraham offered up Isaac. This is the first-fruits of the way being prepared for the restoration of heaven and earth being joined together in one. It will culminate in fullness at His return from heaven to this planet to take up His throne as King of Jerusalem and all nations. In that day, His love will be completely manifest.

In the meantime, the Lord calls us to love the Great King of Jerusalem with all of our heart, soul, mind and strength.

Holiness; the Holy City

The prophet Isaiah saw the Lord while he worshiped in the temple. Around the Lord's throne were seraphim, who worshiped the Lord, saying:

> "Holy, holy, holy is the Lord Almighty; the whole earth is full of His glory" (Isaiah 6:3).

As God's presence was manifest in the temple, Isaiah saw his own unworthiness compared to God's holiness and cried out:

> "Woe to me!" I cried. "I am ruined! For I am a man of unclean lips, and I live among a people of unclean lips, and my eyes have seen the King, the Lord Almighty" (v.4)

If we really have a revelation of the holy King of Jerusalem, the Lord of hosts, we will be undone. Isaiah often refers to God as the "Holy One of Israel." The Holy One of Israel is the Father, Son and Holy Spirit, the Lord our God who is one, the King of Jerusalem.

In the Bible, Jerusalem is referred to as the Holy City, but in many ways today it is an extremely unholy place. Until the Jews, Arabs and others living in this city embrace the Holy One and become partakers of His holiness, there will be no peace in Jerusalem and it will not be a holy city in reality. But praise God that this day is coming soon!

> "On that day HOLY TO THE LORD will be inscribed on the bells of the horses, and the cooking pots in the LORD's house will be like the sacred bowls in front of the altar. Every pot in Jerusalem and Judah will be holy to the LORD Almighty" (Zechariah 14:20-21).

Zechariah 8 says the mountain of the Lord God Almighty will be called the holy mountain. Pray that the Jews and Arabs will truly become partakers of Messiah's holiness and pray for and help each other so that peace, *shalom*, may truly come from heaven to Jerusalem, preparing the way for the Lord.

> "Then I saw a new heaven and a new earth, for the first heaven and the first earth had passed away, and there was no longer any sea. I saw the Holy City, the new Jerusalem, coming down out of heaven from God, prepared as a bride beautifully dressed for her husband" (Revelation 21:1-2).

The Lord, Our Righteousness

The King of Jerusalem is altogether righteous. Isaiah says the Messiah will reign on David's throne and over his kingdom, establishing and upholding it with justice and righteousness, from that time on and forevermore.

> "For to us a child is born, to us a son is given, and the government will be on his shoulders. And he will be called Wonderful Counsellor, Mighty God, Everlasting Father, Prince of Peace. Of the increase of his government and peace there will be no end. He will reign on David's throne and over his kingdom, establishing and upholding it with justice and righteousness from that time on and forever. The zeal of the LORD will accomplish this" (Isaiah 9:6-7).

The first time Jerusalem is mentioned in the Bible, it is associated with righteousness. Abraham met Melchizedek (whose name means "king of righteousness" or "the righteous king") here. Melchizedek was king in the city called Salem, a shortened version of Jerusalem. Salem is derived from the Hebrew word *shalom*, meaning peace, wholeness, completeness and perfection. *Jeru* is a Hebrew root word and from it come several words such as: **to teach, teachings, law, shooting** and **laying a foundation.** It includes actions with a vertical movement (directed from above going downward) and also horizontal movement. Jesus, the Prince of Peace, **coming down** from heaven to earth, born in Bethlehem, crucified in Jerusalem, **ascended** from the Mount of Olives. He will return to the Mount of Olives again and to the eternal Jerusalem, being **sent down** from heaven. Secondly, from Jerusalem the Gospel went out and will go out in the millennium: the horizontal movement. God chose this place on earth to lay down, to cast down, the foundation of His plan of salvation, His way of bringing peace between man and Himself. The word Jerusalem literally means "inheritance of peace." This means that there is peace in the place where the King of righteousness rules and reigns. Pray that the King of righteousness will be accepted by the people of Jerusalem, so they can receive the fullness of inheritance of peace and wholeness. They will never experience their full natural or spiritual inheritance until they recognize and receive their Great King. Also, Isaiah 19:24 describes Israel as God's inheritance.

The King of Jerusalem is also "The Lord our Righteousness." The Messiah is the righteous Branch and the righteous One. He will also usher in everlasting righteousness when He takes up His throne in Jerusalem. His throne will be upheld with righteousness and justice. The Psalms say that there are none righteous. Only God is righteous, because all of us have sinned and fallen short of His glory. In Romans 5, God calls us to be partakers of his righteousness. He is calling us to be slaves to righteousness, leading to holiness.

By faith, Abraham obeyed and went to the place he would receive as an inheritance (Heb. 11:8). He was righteous because he became an heir of the righteousness of the King of Jerusalem. Because of his faith he was counted as righteous (Gen. 15:6).

When the King of Righteousness is restored to Jerusalem, the city will become righteous again.

In Zechariah 9:9, the daughters of Zion are encouraged to rejoice greatly, and the daughters of Jerusalem are to shout because the King is coming to Jerusalem. He is the righteous King who brings salvation. When He comes to set up His throne in Jerusalem, He promises to:

> "... defend my house against marauding forces. Never again will an oppressor overrun my people, for now I am keeping watch" (Zechariah 9:8).

> "For Zion's sake I will not keep silent, for Jerusalem's sake I will not remain quiet, till her righteousness shines out like the dawn, her salvation like a blazing torch. The nations will see your righteousness and all kings your glory" (Isaiah 62:1-2).

Psalms 45 says the Lord loves righteousness and hates wickedness. The world is filled with much wickedness today. But the day is soon coming when the Lord our Righteousness, the King of Jerusalem, will be released from heaven and take up the throne of King David. Because of faith in Him, His people will be partakers of His righteousness. All nations will see His righteousness and all Kings His glory.

Until all Jews and Arabs become partakers of the King's righteousness, they cannot inherit His *shalom/salaam*, His peace.

> "But with righteousness he will judge the needy, with justice he will give decisions for the poor of the earth. He will strike the earth with the rod of his mouth; with the breath of his lips he will slay the wicked" (Isaiah 11:4).

In I Corinthians 1:30, Paul writes that Jesus Christ has become for us "wisdom from God—that is, our righteousness, holiness and redemption." Proverbs 28:1 teaches us that the righteous are as bold as a lion, but the wicked flees though no one pursues.

Justice

In Isaiah 9, the prophet teaches that the throne of David will be established on and upheld with righteousness and justice. God is a God of justice in a world of much injustice.

> **"He has showed you, O man, what is good and what does the Lord require of you? To act justly and to love mercy and to walk humbly with your God" (Micah 6:8).**

There is much injustice between the Jews and the Arabs in the Middle East. Many Arabs have been mistreated and live on a much lower standard than the average Jewish person. Many have had their property taken away from them. The Jewish people should treat those that live among them as their own flesh and blood. This is God's way of justice (Ezek. 47:22).

The Arab people, the sons of Ishmael who have been blessed by God, should treat the Jewish people justly as well, recognizing that the just God established His covenant with Abraham through Isaac. This is *just* because God is a God of justice. They should embrace this covenant and be reconciled as one new man with the Jews in Messiah.

God defends the widow and the fatherless. If we are carrying the Father's heart for the peace of Jerusalem, we need to pray for and help the widows, the fatherless and orphans and do justice to them. We need to pray for the Jews and Arabs to recognize and embrace God as a just God and to treat each other justly.

God will despise and reject our worship if our lives lack justice and righteousness:

> **"I hate, I despise your religious feasts; I cannot stand your assemblies. Even though you bring me burnt offerings and grain offerings, I will not accept them. ... Away with the noise of your songs! I will not listen to the music of your harps. But let justice roll on like a river, righteousness like a never-failing stream!" (Amos 5:21-24)**

The Gentle and Patient One

God is very patient. In the description of love in 1 Corinthians 13, the first characteristic is patience. Love is patient. The Bible says that God is love. The King of Jerusalem is very patient as He has been waiting with long patience for the living stones from all nations to be built into the spiritual temple as a habitation of God in the spirit and for the fruit of the earth to come forth.

> "Rejoice greatly, O Daughter of Zion! Shout, Daughter of Jerusalem! See, your king comes to you, righteous and having salvation, gentle and riding on a donkey, on a colt, the foal of a donkey" (Zechariah 9:9).

The nature and character of the King of Jerusalem is not only to be as bold as a lion, but to be gentle and riding on a donkey. About 30 times in the book of Revelation, the King of Jerusalem is described as the Lamb of God. In the same context of the Lion of the tribe of Judah triumphing and the root of David, the Lamb is said to be looking as if it were slain (Rev. 5:4-5). We will behold Him as the Lamb for eternity in the New Jerusalem. There will not be a temple, because the Lamb will be the eternal Temple for His people.

The only other place in the Old Testament where the word "gentle" is used, is where Elijah sits in a cave, discouraged after Jezebel threatened to kill him (I Kings 19:12). The Lord speaks to him in a gentle whispering voice, to woo him out of the cave and back into God's calling on his life. Many times we miss hearing God's voice and do not respond to Him, because we are not sensitive. God, the Holy Spirit, often speaks to us in a still small voice. Unless we know the nature and character of God and His gentleness, we can miss what He wants to say to us.

> "Come to me, all you who are weary and burdened, and I will give you rest. Take my yoke upon you and learn from me, for I am gentle and humble in heart, and you will find rest for your souls. For my yoke is easy and my burden is light" (Matthew 11:28-30).

If we are going to take on the yoke of the Lord and learn of Him, we not only need to be as bold as lions, but as gentle as lambs and with a humble heart find rest in Him. It is good to know that our Messiah is gentle and patient in the midst of the ruthless and impatient world in which we live. For peace to come to Jerusalem, we need to take on the nature and character of the Messiah and His gentleness, His humble and patient heart. If we do, we will find rest and *shalom* (peace) in our souls and in the city of Jerusalem.

The Compassionate God

> "The LORD came down in the cloud and stood there with [Moses] and proclaimed his name, the LORD. And he passed in front of Moses, proclaiming, 'The LORD, the LORD, the compassionate and gracious God, slow to anger, abounding in love and faithfulness, maintaining love to thousands, and forgiving wickedness, rebellion and sin'" (Exodus 34:5-7).

When Moses met the Lord on the top of Mount Sinai, the Lord came down in a cloud and stood there with him. He passed in front of Moses and proclaimed who He is. The first characteristic of the Lord mentioned is His compassion and graciousness. If true peace is to come to Jerusalem, the fullness of the compassion of the Lord will need to be released through His people to those who have not yet put their trust in Messiah, the Prince of Peace. His kindness is everlasting and endures throughout all generations. The Lord was kind at the flood. The Lord is kind today. He is the same yesterday, today and forever.

> "When he saw the crowds, he had compassion on them, because they were harassed and helpless, like sheep without a shepherd" (Matthew 9:36).

At the age of 85, Derek Prince told me that the Lord released in him a well of compassion for people that he had never had before. May God release this same well in a multitude of people that His heart may be seen in Jerusalem and the surrounding nations. Then we will be able to truly comfort His people.

"Comfort, comfort ye my people, says your God. Speak tenderly to Jerusalem, and proclaim to her that her hard service has been completed, that her sin has been paid for, that she has received from the LORD's hand double for all her sins" (Isaiah 40:1-2).

"But you, O LORD, sit enthroned forever; your renown endures through all generations. You will arise and have compassion on Zion, for it is time to show favor to her; the appointed time has come" (Psalm 102:12-13).

God, Perfect in Beauty

"The Mighty One, God, the Lord, speaks and summons the earth from the rising of the sun to the place where it sets. From Zion, perfect in beauty, our God shines forth" (Psalm 50:1-2).

Beauty has been counterfeited by Satan, and many people have been deceived by the counterfeit. Satan himself appears as a beautiful angel of light (Ezek. 28:6-7).

Genesis 3 says the fruit of the Tree of the Knowledge of Good and Evil was pleasing to the eye, yet it was forbidden. If Adam and Eve had not partaken of this tree, they would have been perfected in beauty by partaking of the Tree of Life. Many people are deceived by the demonic beauty of pornography, experiences while on drugs, and other demonic things of this world. Psalm 50 says God shines forth, perfect in beauty, from Zion. Perfect, Godly beauty is only found in beholding God and as we allow Him to shine through us. Jerusalem's beauty will only be realized in these last days as God is fully perfected in and through His people in Jerusalem. Jerusalem will only fully be perfected in beauty when the Lord Himself returns and shines forth in fullness.

The Eternal God

God is the eternal God who was and is and is to come. The fact that He is eternal means that He has always existed. Because of His eternal love, He decided to create a world to share His love with. When He created the world, He purposed that He as the eternal God would continue in His eternal quest to have a people for Himself. He decided to go on this course, even though He knew He would be rejected, despised, dishonored, blasphemed, ignored, quenched and killed by those He had created in His own image to worship and enjoy Him forever.

While the first Adam failed, the last Adam has triumphed over death, hell and the grave and will usher in eternity. The last Adam, the eternal Adam who is God the Son, came into the world to bring eternal life to those who fell with the first Adam. He is coming back to reign on the Temple Mount for eternity. The first Adam was finite, the last is infinite. The Lord says He will establish a new heaven and a new earth, where will dwell righteousness and holiness for eternity.

Jerusalem will not become an eternal city on earth and in reality until the High and Holy One who inhabits eternity takes up His throne here, puts all things under His feet and brings down the Holy City, the new Jerusalem, out of heaven. Then He will begin His reign in justice and righteousness and holiness in the new heavens and the new earth for eternity.

Pray for the peace of Jerusalem, that the eternal God will soon come to make Jerusalem the eternal city and that all things in heaven and earth will be reconciled in Messiah forever.

Yahweh Shammah (The Lord Is There)

"The name of the city from that time on will be: 'The Lord is There'" (Ezekiel 48:35).

In Jerusalem's final restoration from that time on, the name of the city will be "The Lord is there." The Hebrew translation of this new name, *Yahweh Shammah*, is a wordplay on the Hebrew pronunciation of Jerusalem, *Yerushalayim*. While God is omnipresent, we know that in the center of the Garden of Eden, before the Fall, the Lord's manifest presence was there in a special way. The Lord God could be heard walking in the Garden of Eden in the cool of the day (Gen. 3:8); He was (I am who I am) a blazing torch in the garden and to Moses God appeared as a blazing torch in the burning bush.

The Lord also appears as a blazing torch in Genesis 15:17. There is a need for a *menorah* (lampstand) until separation of the heaven and earth will be restored when the new Jerusalem is filled with the light of His presence.

It is also clear that God's manifest presence was in Jerusalem when Solomon's temple was finished, as the worshipers could not even stand up. His glorious presence was manifest in such a strong way that they had no option but to prostrate themselves before the Great King. Truly, God was there.

When Yeshua puts His feet on the Mount of Olives and the Lord Himself takes up His throne on the Temple Mount in Jerusalem, the Lord will be there in fullness of glory in a greater way than ever before. The name of the city from that time on will be "The Lord is there" because He will remain there forever. His people will also dwell in the land, never to be uprooted again, as a blazing torch at His coming.

The 12 tribes and the 12 gates will be fully restored. His manifest presence will fill Jerusalem and the Temple Mount as the Lamb will be the temple (Rev. 21:22). The earth will be filled with the knowledge of the glory of the Lord as the waters cover the seas.

God Is Good and Merciful

When the Lord appeared to Moses, and Moses asked to see His glory, the Lord said,

> **"'I will cause all my goodness to pass in front of you, and I will proclaim my name, the LORD, in your presence. I will have mercy on whom I will have mercy, and I will have compassion on whom I will have compassion. But,' he said, 'You cannot see my face, for no man may see me and live'" (Exodus 33:19-20).**

The Lord's goodness is so great that the Lord had to place Moses in a cleft in the Rock and cover him with His hand until He passed by. His goodness is so great that Moses would not have been able to survive it. In the same way, when Solomon's Temple on the Temple Mount was filled with God's manifest presence, the goodness of the Lord knocked the priests down and out. At this time, they all declared, "Give thanks to the Lord, for He is good." This was not a cliché, but resulted from a dramatic encounter with a great manifestation of the goodness of God. Out of this context, they said, "**We give thanks to the Lord, for He is good and His mercy endures forever.**" His goodness could have killed them if He had not been merciful to them, keeping them alive as He manifested Himself to them in power and glory as *Yahweh Shammah*, the God who is there. How much greater will His manifest presence and glory be when the Lord Himself takes up his throne in Jerusalem and reigns in fullness of glory; when the city's name is changed forever to "The Lord is there;" and when the Lord takes up the throne of David and reigns in the fullness of His manifest presence as the King of Jerusalem and all nations forever. To pray for the peace of Jerusalem ultimately means to pray for the hastening and the fullness of the changing of the name of the city to *Yahweh Shammah*, which will happen when Messiah comes.

The Lord's goodness leads us to repentance. He has also promised to purge Zion from all filth. This He will do by drawing the people of Zion to Himself by His goodness. If we really experience even a partial revelation of God's goodness, we will be led to repentance. We will see how meaningless life is without the goodness of God. Adam and Eve entered into a big deception when they partook of the Tree of the Knowledge of Good and Evil. They were deceived by Satan when he tricked them into partaking of a counterfeit that blocked their way to the Tree of Life. To partake of the Tree of Life is to partake of all the goodness of God. There is no evil in the Tree of Life.

David said,

"Surely goodness and mercy shall follow me all the days of my life; and I will dwell in the house of the LORD forever" **(Psalm 23:6 NKJV).**

As we live in days of restoration and the Lord is restoring His house in Jerusalem for all nations to stream into, let us be found as faithful watchmen, taking no rest day or night until Jerusalem is established as a praise in the earth. Pray for the peace of Jerusalem, for the fullness of His goodness and mercy to be restored and manifested here in Messiah. All those that love her will prosper.

Chapter 3

Jerusalem, City of the Great King —Blood Sacrifice to Salvation

The capital city of Israel is and has been known by many names in many languages: City of Gold, City of Peace, *Yerushalayim* to the Jews; *Al Quds* to the Arabs; and Aelia Capitolina to the ancient Romans. The variety of names indicate how many times this city has changed hands as civilization upon civilization strived to make the city its own. Tens of thousands of souls have been slaughtered because of Jerusalem.

Jerusalem emerges as a city with a long and complex history to those who look at it with natural eyes to understand its politics, geography and known history. Although its name means "Inheritance of *Shalom* (Peace)," over the last three millennia it has been the center of more conflict, sieges and battles than any other city in the history of the world. Jerusalem has been razed and rebuilt almost 20 times.

The primary reason for the continual conflict over Jerusalem is because Satan knows that *shalom* (peace) will come to the whole world through the sacrifice and atonement of Messiah in Jerusalem. Satan is trying as much as possible to bring confusion and conflict through the anti-Messiah to prevent God's purposes for the city.

Jerusalem was chosen by God as a place of sacrifice and atonement. It is the place where God's manifest presence hovered first in the Garden of Eden (which may have been centered in this part of the Middle East), then over David's tabernacle and later over Solomon's temple. But above all these stands God's declaration that Jerusalem is His own, belonging especially to Him. It is the City of the Great King. It is the city designed and built by God Himself as a tangible representation of the way the Creator has chosen to interact with His creatures. It is the city destined to reveal God's way of salvation for Jew and Gentile through the death and resurrection of Jesus, and also to reveal the new Jerusalem—that glorious place where the fellowship that once existed between the Creator and His creatures in the Garden of Eden will be restored.

> "Again, you have heard that it was said ... long ago, 'Do not break your oath, but keep the oaths you have made to the Lord.' But I tell you, Do not swear at all: either by heaven, for it is God's throne; or by the earth, for it is his footstool; or by Jerusalem, for it is the city of the Great King" (Matthew 5:33-35).

In ancient days, it was customary to swear on something of great value when a person made a promise or entered into an agreement. Words were weighed by the importance of what a person swore on, and oaths were taken very seriously. The Pharisees developed very elaborate systems of vows. Only oaths which invoked heaven or the attributes of God were considered binding. One was to swear by heaven, because it is the throne of God. The second is the earth, because it is God's footstool, and the third is Jerusalem. It is interesting that the Pharisees used Jerusalem as a basis for swearing oaths, and even more so to see the status which Jesus Himself gives to the city, calling it the "City of the Great King."

Each major world religion claims the city as its own. World powers have fought over the city for thousands of years. Within the complex sphere of modern international politics, Jerusalem continues to occupy center stage. Different factions argue over the right to control not only the holy places of its past but also its place in the political future.

Ultimately, however, Jerusalem is important not because of what world religions or heads of state say about it. It is not significant because of its location or its financial wealth. Jerusalem is important because it is the City of the Great King. Jesus Himself chose Jerusalem as the place of world redemption where His ultimate purposes of His death and resurrection and the restoration of the world will be revealed. Jesus will return to earth on the Mount of Olives and from there He will ride through the Golden Gate into the city. On the Temple Mount, He will begin His triumphant eternal reign.

Jesus Revealed in Jerusalem

Jerusalem is an extremely beautiful city. One has only to watch the sun rise over the rooftops of Jerusalem's Old City to be astonished by the wonder, the charm and the mystery of this place. But the city has come to represent something that is much greater than its physical and aesthetic qualities would warrant. One could say that Jerusalem has been elevated and idolized to supernatural importance.

Jerusalem was not created to be worshiped or adored as a city. Rather, the city was created as a lens through which to view God's plans and through which we can get to know the Great King. We could say that Jerusalem is the gateway, or highway, to heaven. The Jews liken praying from the earthly Jerusalem to making a local phone call to the heavenly Jerusalem. The moment we lose sight of the Lord God Almighty, the Father, Jesus the Messiah and the Holy Spirit, we lose sight of the eternal meaning of Jerusalem.

The following are ten different ways in which Jesus has revealed Himself and His plan for the eternal new Jerusalem in the Scriptures. Nine have already taken place, and one is yet to come.

The First Revelation:
Jesus Revealed in the Person of Melchizedek

> "By faith Abraham, when called to go to a place he would later receive as his inheritance, obeyed and went, even though he did not know where he was going. By faith he made his home in the promised land like a stranger in a foreign country; he lived in tents, as did Isaac and Jacob, who were heirs with him of the same promise. For he was looking forward to the city with foundations, whose architect and builder is God" (Hebrews 11:8-10).

Here we read how Abraham went out from Ur of the Chaldees. Abraham left his home and set out on a journey into the unknown by faith alone. He left for a place that he would later receive as an inheritance, even though he did not know where he was going. By faith, he made his home in the Promised Land and lived like a stranger in a foreign country. He lived in temporary tents, and so did Isaac and Jacob after him. They were heirs with him of the same promises.

Despite the barren desert around him, Abraham continued to believe in the promises of God for him. He looked for that **"city with foundations, whose architect and builder is God."** When Abraham set out, he wasn't looking for the physical Jerusalem (it did not exist yet) but for something even more important—a city with eternal foundations, built and designed by God Himself. With eyes of faith, Abraham was looking for the heavenly Jerusalem, whose builder and maker is God Himself.

Where did Abraham finally find himself? In the earthly Jerusalem. He was willing to follow the voice of the Lord wherever it took him, and he found himself as close as he could ever hope to be to the heavenly Jerusalem. And when he arrived there, who did he meet? He met the great high priest and king of the city of Salem, Melchizedek, whose name means righteous king (Gen. 14:18). *Salem*, which is the Aramaic word for peace, was the first name of the city of Jerusalem. This word very closely resembles the Hebrew and Arabic words for peace—*shalom* and *salaam* respectively. When Abraham arrived in the city, the king of peace greeted him. The king was so great, and inspired so much reverence, that Abraham paid tribute to him by giving him a tenth of his goods.

Melchizedek was a great man, described as one **"made like the Son of God" (Hebrews 7:3-4).** He very well may have been the person of the Lord Jesus. In the book of Daniel, when a mysterious stranger appeared to Shadrach, Meshach, and Abednego after they had been thrown into the fiery furnace, they said that this being was "like the Son of God." I believe the Lord Jesus was in their midst then. Abraham probably had a personal encounter with the Lord Jesus when he came to Jerusalem.

Melchizedek, the high priest, then offered him bread and wine. What was the significance of this? We know that the bread and wine represent the covenant between God and man. It represents the body of Jesus that was broken for us, and His blood that was shed for us. This is the first time that bread, wine and the city of Jerusalem are mentioned in the Bible. Thousands of years before Jesus ever walked the earth, He appeared to Abraham in Jerusalem as the King of Salem, the King of Jerusalem. He greeted him, and took communion with him. Jesus said, **"Abraham rejoiced at the thought of seeing my day; he saw it and was glad"** (John 8:56).

Abraham saw the day of the Lord when he died. But he saw beyond that. He saw the new Jerusalem coming down out of heaven, the city whose builder and maker is God. Jerusalem was created to reveal the person of the Lord Jesus and, if we lose this as our focus, the city will become an idol.

The Second Revelation: The Sacrifice of Jesus Revealed Through the Sacrifice of Isaac

In Genesis 22, God told Abraham to take his son to Mount Moriah, later called Mount Zion, the location where the temple in Jerusalem was later constructed. There, Abraham was to sacrifice his only son, the child of the promise. This sacrifice of Isaac was a foreshadowing of the sacrifice that Jesus, the Son of God, would make for the sins of the world. Abraham's willingness to obey, even to the death of his son, indicated a willingness to follow God with his whole heart. God was not interested in Isaac's death. Rather, he was concerned with Abraham's obedience. Isaac would not have been an acceptable sacrifice, for he was not without sin. God did not make a promise to give Abraham a son only to take it back. At the last minute, a ram came out of the thicket and was offered up as a blood sacrifice, foretelling the coming of the Lord Jesus who would be the ultimate, and totally acceptable, offering for our sins.

The Third Revelation: Freedom from Slavery—Egypt and Sin— Revealed in Jerusalem by Blood Sacrifice

The third revelation we have of Jerusalem is in the departure of the Jewish people from Egypt after 400 years of slavery. Where did these people go? They headed to Jerusalem because God destined them to become a nation. As in previous incidents, several common themes can be identified. Blood sacrifice, the blood spread on the lintels of all Jewish homes to protect them from the angel of death. (The marks made on the lintels with the

blood, form a cross, interestingly enough.) It points forward to the sacrifice of Jesus that would take place 1,300 years later in Jerusalem. One
generation of Israelites died in the wilderness because they were unwilling
to follow the Lord with all their hearts and to believe in His promises. In
Exodus 3:16-17, God spoke to Moses, saying,

> "Go, assemble the elders of Israel and say to them, 'The LORD,
> the God of your fathers—the God of Abraham, Isaac and Jacob–
> –appeared to me and said: "I have watched over you and have
> seen what has been done to you in Egypt. And I have promised
> to bring you up out of your misery in Egypt into the land of
> the Canaanites, Hittites, Amorites, Perizzites, Hivites, and
> Jebusites—a land flowing with milk and honey."'"

The Promised Land was the Israelites' physical inheritance. But its capital,
Jerusalem, pointed the way to their spiritual inheritance in their Messiah
who lived, died and rose from the dead in Jerusalem.

The Fourth Revelation:
The Body of Messiah
Revealed As the Ark of God

The fourth way that the Lord revealed Himself was when David brought the
ark back to Jerusalem. The ark represents the presence of God, which had
been removed from His people. Before the death and resurrection of Messiah Jesus, God's presence dwelled in the Ark of the Covenant, which was
a tangible reminder of His presence among His people. Today, God dwells
in His people. The Body of Messiah throughout the world has become the
ark of God.

In I Chronicles 15, we read how David brought the ark back to Jerusalem. He saw how God blessed the temporary resting place of the ark and
believed that he needed to bring it to Jerusalem and make it its permanent
home. Because this was eventually done in God's timing and in God's way,
they triumphantly marched into Jerusalem. When the presence of God is
with us and He is watching over us, then no one can be against us. If our
hearts are totally committed to Him, He will be with us just as he was with

David as he brought the ark into Jerusalem. When the priests brought the ark to the tabernacle that David had made for it (I Chron. 16), they offered sacrifices. They offered bulls and rams, burnt offerings and fellowship offerings, because this was a sign of covenant between God and man. Blood sacrifices were also a foreshadowing of the sacrifice of Jesus. In this instance, the sacrifices looked forward to the time when we, the Body of Messiah on earth, would become the ark of God. Here again, the Lord Jesus is revealed through the city of Jerusalem, with the shedding of sacrificial blood pointing the way to His ultimate sacrifice.

The Fifth Revelation:
The Spiritual Temple Revealed in
the Building of the Physical Temple

The fifth revelation of Jerusalem is in II Chronicles 7. Solomon had just finished building his magnificent temple, and the people were gathered to dedicate the house of the Lord. One can only imagine the jubilation that filled the hearts of the people the day that the temple, the house of God, was finally completed. David had prayed to be able to build a house for God, but the task was given to Solomon. (See map 3, page 189.)

The completion of the temple is a picture of something else that is going to happen in the future. Imagine what a glorious day it will be when the last stone is put into the spiritual temple. Solomon's temple was magnificent in itself, but it was also a wonderful picture of something to come because the presence of the Lord dwelt in this temple. The purpose of the first temple was for the worship of God, but the people were still offering up animal sacrifices because the ultimate sacrifice had not yet been made. The temple was to be the site of sacrifice. The sacrifices offered by Solomon were staggering. In total, 22,000 bulls and 120,000 sheep were killed on one day as sacrificial offerings for the Lord; these pointed ahead to Yeshua. He became the ultimate Lamb slain so that the need for animal sacrifice forever was done away with; although, in the millennial temple of Ezekiel, there may be animal sacrifices for a short time. He is building the most glorious temple out of living stones that will last for eternity (see Rev. 21).

The Sixth Revelation:
First-Fruits of the New Jerusalem
Foreshadowed in Jesus' Birth

The sixth foreshadowing of Jerusalem lies in the story of Jesus' birth. In fulfillment of prophecy, Jesus was born in Bethlehem, on the outskirts of Jerusalem. In this historic moment, the Word became flesh and tabernacled among us. Jesus came into the world to show us how to live, and to die for our sins that we might live eternally with Him. You could say that His birth is the first-fruit of the reconciliation of all things and heaven and earth becoming one in the new Jerusalem. His second coming is the fullness. At His first coming He tabernacled as the Lamb of God, but in His second coming He will tabernacle as the Lion of the tribe of Judah.

The Bible tells us that in the beginning was the Word, and that the Word was made flesh and dwelt among us. Time is not based around Buddha, Mohammed or Confucius. God created time, and inserted Himself into time at His chosen moment. Most of the world divides the calendar into the years before Christ and after Christ (AD stands for *Anno Domino*, or the Year of Our Lord).

It is interesting to remember how, just as Pharaoh killed all young boys at the time of the birth of Moses, so did King Herod order the massacre of all Jewish boys under the age of two around the time of Messiah's birth. Here we can see how the enemy was trying to wipe out God's destiny for Jerusalem as the City of the Great King Jesus by trying to destroy the newly born Savior of the world. In the same way, the enemy will raise up an anti-Christ in the last days to try to confuse and persecute all who are looking forward to the return of Messiah.

The Seventh Revelation:
Jesus' Death and Resurrection
Reveals God's Plan of Restoration

The seventh significant area in the revelation of Jerusalem is the account of the death and resurrection of Jesus. In about 33 AD, Jesus was crucified in

Jerusalem. He came to reveal Himself to His people and to die for the sins of the whole world:

> "He did not enter by means of the blood of goats and calves; but he entered the Most Holy Place once for all by his own blood, having obtained eternal redemption. The blood of goats and bulls and the ashes of a heifer sprinkled on those who are ceremonially unclean sanctify them so that they are outwardly clean. How much more, then, will the blood of Christ, who through the eternal Spirit offered himself unblemished to God, cleanse our consciences from acts that lead to death, so that we may serve the living God!" (Hebrews 9:12-15)

The blood of Jesus was offered up in Jerusalem for our sins as a complete sacrifice, the only blood sacrifice that was totally acceptable to God. There is no more need for animal sacrifices. If you ask the Jewish people today, they do not know how to address the issue of animal sacrifices. However, we know what to tell them because the blood of Jesus was offered up for all the world. Not only did Jesus die in Jerusalem, He rose from the dead in that very city, and revealed Himself to His disciples there. After He ascended into heaven, the Holy Spirit was poured out on His disciples in Jerusalem, and then on the rest of the world.

The Eighth Revelation:
Jesus' Discipline and Judgment Revealed

Jesus prophesied that both the temple and Jerusalem were going to be totally destroyed. Luke 21:20-24 indicates that Jerusalem will be surrounded by armies:

> "When you see Jerusalem being surrounded by armies, you will know that its desolation is near. Then let those who are in Judea flee to the mountains, let those in the city get out, and let those in the country not enter the city. For this is the time of punishment in fulfillment of all that has been written. How dreadful it will be in those days for pregnant women and nursing mothers! There will be great distress in the land and wrath against this people. They will fall by the sword and will be taken as prison-

ers to all the nations. Jerusalem will be trampled on by the Gentiles until the times of the Gentiles are fulfilled."

Here, Jesus prophesied the destruction of Jerusalem that occurred 40 years, or one generation, after He began to preach the Gospel. Jesus wept over Jerusalem and declared:

> "O Jerusalem, Jerusalem, you who kill the prophets and stone those sent to you, how often I have longed to gather your children together, as a hen gathers her chicks under her wings, but you were not willing. Look, your house is left to you desolate. For I tell you, you will not see me again until you say, 'Blessed is he who comes in the name of the LORD'" (Matthew 23:37).

In chapter 24, as He is leaving the Holy Temple, He says that not one stone will be left standing on another. Every stone will be overturned.

In 70 AD, almost 40 years after Jesus died, the Lord revealed Himself again. This time, however, He did not come watching over His people with love and compassion in His heart. He revealed Himself as a God of discipline and judgment. Scripture reminds us that He who watches over Israel neither slumbers nor sleeps, so we know that the destruction of Jerusalem by the Roman soldiers did not go unnoticed by God. It was not a tragedy that "slipped by" when God was looking the other direction. When we are walking with God, following His commandments, and enjoying honest fellowship with Him, He watches over us protectively. If we rebel against God continually, we find ourselves on the receiving end of the chastisement of God. In 70 AD, the temple was destroyed, Jerusalem was razed, and those Jews who were not murdered were scattered to the four corners of the earth. It was a curse to the Jews because they were uprooted from their own land and scattered among the nations, where many did not want to receive them.

Those among the exiled who knew Jesus as their Messiah took the Gospel with them. The first missionaries were Jewish believers who took the Gospel to the Gentiles in the lands where they found homes. One could say that the destruction of Jerusalem and subsequent scattering of the Jews were a blessing for the Gentiles, because it brought them the good news of salvation.

The destruction of the Holy Temple in Jerusalem and the dispersion of the Jews marked the end of animal sacrifices although some believe there is a possibility of that being restored for a short while in the new millennium. The words of Jesus came true literally within 40 years after He died, 40 years or almost a generation after He prophesied, and 70 years from the time of His birth.

The Ninth Revelation: The First-Fruits of Jerusalem's Redemption and Restoration

The Spirit of the Lord brooded over the earth for a long time, for the ninth revelation of Jerusalem did not take place until 1967. The revelation had been in a state of preparation since the beginning of the 20th Century, for it was then that the Jews started returning to the land of their fathers from the four corners of the earth. In 1948, Israel was reborn as a nation but Jerusalem itself remained in Arab hands. In speaking of the destruction of Jerusalem, Jesus Himself told us that **"Jerusalem will be trampled on by the Gentiles until the times of the Gentiles are fulfilled" (Luke 21: 24).** In June 1967, Israeli paratroopers came through the Lions Gate and recaptured East Jerusalem and the Old City, including the Temple Mount. The paratroopers who broke through the walls immediately rushed to the wall to pray and in the days immediately following this event, soldiers and civilians from all over Israel streamed to the wall to pray once again at this most holy place. Grown men, soldiers, women and children wept at this wall which represents the prayers, heart cries and deepest longings of the Jewish people throughout the centuries.

Prior to June 1967, Jerusalem had been like the city of Berlin, a city divided by a wall that was impossible to breach. In Berlin, those who tried to get over the wall were brutally killed and their bodies left to rot in the open as a reminder to others foolish enough to think that they could find a way across to the other side. In Jerusalem as well, it was impossible to go back and forth between the different sectors of the city. Jews could not go through the Arab quarter to pray at the wall; the holy place was completely inaccessible to the Jews, even though it was physically just a short distance from where many of them lived and worked in Jerusalem. The Old City, the Mount of Olives and the area surrounding the Western Wall used to be part of the nation of Jordan. It was a different country altogether, under Arab rule, and not open to the Jewish people.

Now, for the first time in thousands of years, Jerusalem is a city united once again under Jewish rule; furthermore, and despite international political opposition, Jerusalem was declared the official capital of the nation of Israel.

I have had the privilege of living in Jerusalem for 13 years, since 1987, and there is no place in the world that I love more than this city. Over time, Jesus has given me increasingly His heart for this city. I have lived among the Jewish people in West Jerusalem and among the Arabs in East Jerusalem, and each group is of great value in the sight of the Lord. When I first moved to Jerusalem, my ministry was primarily directed to Jewish people. When I began to look for a house of prayer, I started looking in West Jerusalem, but I felt that the Lord was directing me to the Mount of Olives. I was puzzled and asked him, "Lord, are you sure you are not making a mistake?" But as we have been living and working there, our hearts have been filled with a deep love for the Arab families who surround us, and we have come to a deeper understanding of God's ultimate intention to break down the wall of partition between Arab and Jew. In Jesus, there is neither Arab nor Jew. His blood has been shed for all mankind, regardless of race or gender, and His purpose is to unite all people in the person of Jesus the Messiah. This is beginning to happen.

Because of its strategic importance in the purposes of God for the last days, the spiritual warfare over Jerusalem is overwhelming. Even as this book is being written, it is imperative that believers around the world be praying against the spirit that tries to divide Jerusalem politically, personally and spiritually. It is of the greatest importance that Jewish and Arab pastors continue to pray and seek God together. Over the past ten years, we have been coordinating meetings between Jewish and Arab pastors in Jerusalem. It is deeply encouraging to see that things are progressing spiritually as individuals from both sides are receiving Messiah and are being reconciled in Him. Reconciliation in Messiah is our only hope for peace until the Prince of Peace takes up His throne in this city.

Just as God began to move physically in the reunification of Jerusalem, He began to act spiritually. Jesus tells His disciples to look at the fig tree as it begins to sprout:

> **"Look at the fig tree and all the trees. When they sprout leaves, you can see for yourselves and know that summer is near. Even so, when you see these things happening, you know that the Kingdom of God is near" (Luke 21:29-31).**

One of the signs that the Lord Jesus is coming soon, is the great revival taking place in the nations and among the Jewish people. In 1967, there were only a few Messianic congregations in the United States and barely a handful in Israel. Today, there are over 600 congregations of Jewish believers in the world. Truly, the fig tree is beginning to blossom.

Several years ago, on the 25th anniversary of the reunification of Jerusalem, the Lord began to show us we needed to pray that, just as the city had become physically liberated and united, this needed to take place also in the spiritual. Jesus died to liberate Jerusalem not only in the natural but also in the spiritual realm. We need to believe that the Muslims in Jerusalem will be liberated from the bondage of Islam and that God will liberate the Jewish people from the blindness that holds them captive.

Everyone is waiting for the Messiah's return. The Jews are looking for Him, and most expect that He will come as a man out of the earth. The anti-Christ will also arise from the powers of this world, and we must be praying that God lift the veil from the eyes of the Jewish people before the arrival of the anti-Christ. The high level of expectations among the Jewish people for a Messiah makes them vulnerable targets for deception masquerading as truth.

Living on the Mount of Olives has given me a fascinating insight into the Muslim heart. Muslims basically believe that Jesus is coming back to the Mount of Olives from heaven. While they believe that Jesus was a prophet and a very good man, and they are looking forward to His return, they do not believe that He is the Son of God. According to their beliefs, when Jesus returns He will go to the mosque located at the Dome of the Rock and the leader of the mosque will offer Him control of the mosque. He will not accept this honor, instead leaving the current leader in charge. However, He will convert to Islam. The Muslims respect Jesus, and so when they hear that we are praying for His return they are happy because they too believe that His return will bring peace.

The Liberation of Jerusalem

"... the women represent two covenants. One covenant is from Mount Sinai and bears children who are to be slaves: This is Hagar. Now Hagar stands for Mount Sinai in Arabia and corresponds to the present city of Jerusalem, because she is in slavery with her children. But the Jerusalem that is above is free, and she is our mother. For it is written:

'Be glad, O barren woman, who bears no children; break forth and cry aloud, you who have no labor pains; because more are the children of the desolate woman than of her who has a husband.'

Now you, brothers, like Isaac, are children of promise. At that time the son born in the ordinary way persecuted the son born by the power of the Spirit. It is the same now. But what does the Scripture say?

'Get rid of the slave woman and her son, for the slave woman's son will never share in the inheritance with the free woman's son.'

Therefore, brothers, we are not children of the slave woman, but of the free woman. It is for freedom that Christ has set us free. Stand firm, then, and do not let yourselves be burdened again by a yoke of slavery" (Galatians 4:24–5:1).

Today, the Lord is speaking this scripture prophetically over Jerusalem. In many ways, Jerusalem still remains in bondage but God wants to bring spiritual liberation to the city of Jerusalem. He wants to cast out religious spirits and wants men and women to be born again by the spirit of God. He wants those who believe in Him to understand His end-time purposes for Jerusalem. He wants to liberate the Muslims from the bondage of the curse put on them, and to liberate the Jews from the spirit of the anti-Christ which seeks to control them and blind them to the truth.

The Tenth Revelation: Jesus To Be Revealed As the Great King of Jerusalem

The tenth revelation of Jerusalem, the one that we have yet to see, is to be found in Zechariah 13:1-2:

> "'On that day a fountain will be opened to the house of David and the inhabitants of Jerusalem, to cleanse them from sin and impurity. On that day, I will banish the names of the idols from the land, and they will be remembered no more,' declares the LORD Almighty. 'I will remove both the prophets and the spirit of impurity from the land.'"

And in Zechariah 14:4:

> "On that day his feet will stand on the Mount of Olives, east of Jerusalem, and the Mount of Olives will be split in two from east to west, forming a great valley, with half of the mountain moving north and half moving south."

> "At that time they will call Jerusalem The Throne of the LORD, and all nations will gather in Jerusalem to honor the name of the LORD. No longer will they follow the stubbornness of their evil hearts" (Jeremiah 3:17).

> "Foreigners will occupy Ashdod, and I will cut off the pride of the Philistines. I will take the blood from their mouths, the forbidden food from between their teeth. Those who are left will belong to our God and become leaders in Judah, and Ekron will be like the Jebusites" (Zechariah 9:6-7).

Chapter 4

A History of Jerusalem, God's Eternal City

1,000 years	Adam to Noah
1,000 years	Noah to Abraham
1,000 years	Abraham to David
1,000 years	David to Jesus
2,000 years	Jesus to 2000 AD

Approximately 4,000 years	Adam to Jesus

Jerusalem is first mentioned in the Bible in Genesis 14:18, when Abraham takes offerings of bread and wine to the priest Melchizedek. Abraham took Isaac to Mount Moriah, which later became the Temple Mount, to sacrifice him. David was called to make Jerusalem the capital of Israel and it was there that Solomon built the magnificent first temple. By that time, Jerusalem had become precious to the hearts of the Jews everywhere in the Promised Land. When they were exiled for the first time, it was over Jerusalem that they mourned and lamented (Psa. 137:1-6). It was to Jerusalem that God commanded all the Jews to make a pilgrimage three times a year for His holy convocations and it was to Jerusalem that Yeshua, our Messiah, came to fulfill His mission of reconciliation and redemption.

Jerusalem is mentioned 657 times in the Hebrew Scriptures and 154 times in the New Testament, or more than 800 times in the complete Bible. Zion is mentioned 157 times in the Hebrew Scriptures and seven times in the New Testament. As a point of contrast, *Al-Quds* (the Arabic name for

Jerusalem which means 'the Holy One') is not even mentioned once in the Koran, the sacred writings of the Muslims. Jerusalem has never in history been the capital of any nation other than the Jews.

The power struggles over Jerusalem throughout history serve as an indication of the importance of this city. Jerusalem is the story of the Fall of man, repentance, reconciliation and restoration. Father Abraham (Gen. 15) represents God's covenant. For the next 6,000 years Arabs (Gentiles) and Jews have struggled over Jerusalem. The struggle will continue until peace is restored in Messiah when He comes. But God is already working already in a powerful way toward the restoration of His purposes for Egypt, Israel and Assyria as Ishmael is being welcomed back in the house by Messianic Jewish believers today. This is a first-fruit of Isaiah 19:23-25.

In the years following the Roman conquest and the expulsion of the Jews from their homeland in 70 AD, the Emperor Constantine declared Christianity to be the religion of the Holy Roman Empire. His mother, Helena, made several pilgrimages to Jerusalem, building churches and monuments over what she believed were the actual sites of events in Jesus' life. The Church of the Holy Sepulchre is one of the most notable, commemorating what Roman Catholics believe to be the site of Jesus' crucifixion and burial. Jerusalem thus became a holy city to Christians. Pilgrims from throughout Europe later risked their fortunes and their lives over long and perilous journeys to retrace the footsteps of Jesus.

In the 7th century AD, Muslims claimed Jerusalem as a sacred site. During the 11th and 12th centuries, the Crusaders attempted to take the Holy City but failed miserably. With the exception of a scraggly and poor remnant of religious Jews who were waiting for the coming of the Messiah, Jerusalem remained in Muslim hands until 1967.

Yet even now, although the city is under Jewish rule, newspapers are filled with intense debates about the final status of Jerusalem. Will Jerusalem also become the capital of a new Palestinian state? Whose Jerusalem is it anyway? Jerusalem has become a gambling chip in peace talks. The city's fate is a key factor in international negotiations. Palestinian Arabs and Jews both claim rights to Jerusalem as their capital, and world pressure is mounting on Israel. It is more important than ever to remind God of His promises that Jerusalem will be Messiah's united capital forever.

God's view of history and His plan are much greater than our perspective and defies even the most creative contemporary imagination. Instead of settling for a series of unsatisfactory and painful compromises, God's plan is to make Jerusalem a united city, where those parties currently opposed to one another, Jews and Arabs, will be reconciled into one new man. In the light of modern events, this seems almost impossible. But with God all things are possible. God's Word will not return to Him void, but will accomplish what He purposes. While the plans of man will cause nothing but dissension and strife, the plans of God are designed to bring blessing to the whole world. This is not a time to keep silent. It is a time for watchmen to arise in worship, intense and committed intercession, and to stand with the Lord for Jerusalem.

Isaiah 62:1 says Jerusalem's salvation will eventually be like a blazing torch. Zechariah 12:6 says the leaders of Judah will be like a firepot in a woodpile and like a flaming torch among sheaves. The bowls of incense of the prayers for the peace of Jerusalem over the last 4,000 to 6,000 years will be brought to fullness by your prayers, bringing the Prince of Peace back to His eternal capital.

A careful reading of the Bible and a biblical understanding of history provide us with a much deeper understanding of the centrality of Jerusalem in God's plan. In Isaiah 62:2, God promises that the nations will see Jerusalem's righteousness and that the city will be called by a new name. We need to have an understanding of what has happened in history, but we need to see that history is a tool in God's hands to fulfill His ultimate promises and purposes for His holy, eternal new Jerusalem, which will come down from heaven and be our home forever.

Strategic Dates in the
4,000-Year History of Jerusalem

Continue praying for the peace of Jerusalem, and restoration of earth and heaven in Messiah until He comes; all those who love her will prosper (Psalm 122:6).

Pre-Biblical and Biblical Periods (2000–538 BC)

20th – 19th century BCE

> *Urusalim* (Jerusalem) is mentioned in Egyptian Execration Texts.

18th century BCE

> The patriarch Abraham is welcomed by Melchizedek, the King and High Priest of Jerusalem. First mention of Jerusalem by name in the Bible. At this time he saw the new Jerusalem, coming down out of heaven with foundations, and whose builder and maker was God! (Heb. 11:10).

13th century BCE

> Joshua captures Canaan, but Jebus (Jerusalem) remains hostile.

1014   David proclaimed King of Judea at Hebron.

 996   King David captures Jerusalem and makes it his capital. Soon afterward he brings the ark to Jerusalem.

 954   King Solomon commences construction of the First Temple.

 930   The kingdom is divided; Jerusalem remains the capital of Judah.

 922   The Egyptian pharaoh, Sheshonk I, sacked the city.

773 – 759

> The reign of King Uzziah, who builds towers and fortifies the city.

 701   Sennacherib, King of Assyria, fails to conquer the city. Isaiah's prophecy that God will turn back the invader is fulfilled. Water for the besieged city is supplied through King Hezekiah's tunnel connecting the Gihon spring with the pool of Siloam.

 626   Jeremiah challenges the priests and is consequently banned from entering the Temple.

605 Babylon defeats Egypt at Carchemish. Jeremiah warns against the "evil from the north," alluding to Nebuchadnezzar's army.

597 King Jehoiakim, his family and Ezekiel exiled to Babylon. The prophet predicts the doom of Judah and envisions the "revival of the dry bones of Israel."

586 Nebuchadnezzar, King of Babylon, captures the city, burns the Temple and exiles the inhabitants to Babylon.

538 King Cyrus' historic edict, allowing Jews to repatriate and start to rebuild the Holy Temple in Jerusalem.

Persian Period (539–332 BC)

520 The construction of the Second Temple under Zerubbabel is encouraged by Zechariah who, in 519, had his messianic visions.

444 The city walls are rebuilt by Nehemiah.

397 Religious reforms by Ezra the scribe.

Hellenistic–Hasmonean Period (320–152 BC)

301 Ptolemy I (a general of Alexander the Great and also his historian) captures Jerusalem. He is the founder of the Ptolemaic dynasty.

198 Antiochus III wrests Jerusalem from the Ptolemaic Greeks.

167 Antiochus IV Epiphanes, the Seleucid Emperor, desecrates the Temple and turns it into a house of idol worship.

164 Following the Hasmonean revolt, Judah the Maccabee liberates Jerusalem and re-consecrates the Temple—an event marked by the festival of Hanukkah.

160 Judah Maccabee falls in the Battle of el-Assa, north of Jerusalem.

152 Jonathan, Judah's brother, takes possession of Jerusalem and is proclaimed High Priest.

Roman Period (70 BC–292 AD)

63 Pompeii lays siege to and captures Jerusalem, putting it under tribute to Rome.

54   Julius Crassus, Roman Governor of Syria, plunders the Temple's treasures in Jerusalem.

20   King Herod I starts reconstructing the Temple, making it one of the most impressive edifices in the Roman Empire. Other magnificent buildings erected during his reign are Herod's Palace and the Antonia Fortress.

4   At the death of King Herod I (the Great), his son Archelaus rules until 6 AD when he is dismissed and exiled by Emperor Augustus.

0–6   The birth of Jesus Christ in Bethlehem, near Jerusalem.

18   Jesus comes to Jerusalem with his parents and exchanges thoughts and ideas with doctors of law in the Temple.

33   Jesus and his disciples come to Jerusalem for the Passover pilgrimage, holding the traditional Seder, later described as the "Last Supper." The next day, Jesus is arrested, tried and crucified by order of the Roman Procurator, Pontius Pilate, fulfilling the prophecies that He is the Passover Lamb, the ultimate sacrifice to take away the sins of the world. Animal sacrifices stop shortly after this time.

• The Holy Spirit was poured out in Jerusalem on the literal day of the Jewish Feast of *Shavuot* (Pentecost). (See Joel 2 and Acts 2.)

• After His resurrection, Jesus ascended into heaven from the Mount of Olives. Before He disappeared, He said to the Jewish people that they would not see Him again until they say: "Blessed is he who comes in the name of the Lord."

35   The apostle Stephen is stoned outside Jerusalem.

66   The start of the Jewish revolt against the Roman occupation. Cestius Gallus, Roman Governor of Syria, fails to capture Jerusalem, and his forces are routed at the gorge of Beth Horon.

• James, Jesus' brother, is martyred in Jerusalem.

68   Vespasian, the Roman general, later to become emperor, conquers the country and hands over command to his son Titus.

70   Titus captures Jerusalem, sets fire to the Temple and destroys the

city. This is one generation after Jesus' birth, and happened just as He prophesied (Matt. 24:1-2).

132 The Jewish revolt against Rome is led by Bar Kochba, and Jerusalem is once more in Jewish hands.

133 Emperor Hadrian crushes the revolt and builds a Roman city on the ruins of Jerusalem. He names it Aelia Capitolina, after the Roman idol, Jupiter Capitolinus, and himself, Publius Aelius Hadrianus. He changes the name of the land from Judea to Palestine.

Byzantine Period (326–638 AD)

326 Helena, mother of Constantine the Great, and said to have found the True Cross, makes her historic visit to Jerusalem.

333 The first Christian pilgrim arrives from Bordeaux, and describes his visit, reporting Jews who come to a "pierced stone" which "they anoint"; "then they mourn and rend their garments."

335 The consecration of the Church of the Holy Sepulchre, built by order of Emperor Constantine.

443–460

Empress Eudocia settles in Jerusalem, builds the Church of St. Stephen and extends the walls. The ban on the Jewish presence in the city is lifted.

530 There are over 26 churches recorded in Jerusalem.

614 The Persians under Khursau II capture Jerusalem assisted by 25,000 Jewish fighters from the Galilee. Jews are allowed to settle in the city. Permission to rebuild the Temple is withdrawn after three years.

629 Byzantine rule is restored by Emperor Heraclius. The relic of the True Cross, which had been taken away by the Persians, is returned to the Church of the Holy Sepulchre.

Early Muslim Period (638–1099 AD)

638 Six years after Mohammed's death, Jerusalem surrenders to Caliph

Omar Ibn al-Khattab, following the Yarmuk battle of 636 where he defeated the Byzantines.

692 Caliph Abd-al-Malik of the Umayyad dynasty (ruling from Damascus) builds the Dome of the Rock, also called the Mosque of Omar.

860 Yeshivat Eretz Israel (Religious Academy) moves from Tiberias to Jerusalem, to become the central authority on Jewish religious law for the country and the western *diaspora*.

878 Egyptian Ahmed Ibn Tulun captures Jerusalem.

900 The Karaite leader, Daniel HaKomsi, urges the *diaspora* (dispersed) Jewish communities to make *aliyah* to Jerusalem.

1010 Caliph al-Hakim destroys synagogues and churches, including the Holy Sepulchre (rebuilt by Emperor Constantine IX, Monomachus 1030–1048).

1055 From southern Germany and Holland, 12,000 pilgrims start an ill-fated journey to Jerusalem, but only a few reach the city.

1071 The Seljuks, an army of Turkish mercenaries, pillage Jerusalem. Their harsh rule and abuse of pilgrims result in the First Crusade.

Crusader Period (1099-1187 AD)

1099 Following Pope Urban II's call in 1096 for a crusade to liberate the holy places, the Crusader army, led by Godfrey, captures Jerusalem and slaughters Jewish and Muslim inhabitants. Godfrey's brother, Baldwin, is crowned King of Jerusalem in Bethlehem in 1101.

1118 The powerful Order of the Templars is founded by Hugh de Payens.

1142 The imposing Church of St. Anne is built at the request of Crusader Queen Arda.

Ayyubid Period (1187-1260 AD)

1187 Saladin (Yussuf Ibn Ayyub of the Ayyubid dynasty), a brilliant Muslim commander of Kurdish descent, captures Jerusalem after defeating the Crusaders at the Horns of Hittin, and allows Jews and Muslims to return to the city.

1192 King Richard, the Lion-hearted, fails to conquer Jerusalem, but signs a status quo agreement with Saladin, guaranteeing Christians access to their holy sites.

1212 Jewish *aliyah* resumes with the simultaneous arrival of 300 rabbis and scholars from France and Britain.

1219 Jerusalem's city walls are razed by order of Malik al-Muazzam, Sultan of Cairo. Jerusalem remains without walls for 322 years.

• St. Francis of Assisi, founder of the Franciscan Order, arrives.

1229 The Crusaders temporarily regain control of Jerusalem through a 10-year treaty signed by Emperor Frederick II of Germany and Sicily and Sultan al-Kamil of Egypt.

1244 An army of Khawarezmian's Turks from Central Asia captures and pillages the city, finally ending Christian rule.

1260 A short-lived capture of Jerusalem by Mongolian chief Hulagi Khan. Scrolls of the Law are moved to Shechem for safety.

• The Mamelukes (descendants of Turkish and Caucasian slave soldiers who had founded a dynasty in Egypt) capture Jerusalem and enrich the city by building many *madrasas* (religious colleges) and *zawiyas* (convents).

Mameluke Period (1260–1516 AD)

1265 Sultan Baybars initiates annual religious procession from Jerusalem to the tomb of *Nebi Mussa* (Prophet Moses) near Jericho. He defeats the Mongols at the Battle of Jalud (Ein-Harod) in 1260.

1267 The great scholar, Nahmanides (the Ramban), and his disciples arrive from Spain. They revive the Jewish community and build the synagogue bearing his name.

1335 Augustine the monk, Jacques of Verona, praises Jewish guides of Jerusalem, noting its long established Jewish community. Ibn Battuta, records pilgrims' complaints of high taxation and humiliation.

1336 The Franciscan Order is appointed custodian of the holy places.

1348 The plague, Black Death, engulfs the city.

1365 Christian monks on Mount Zion deported to Damascus to die in prison there.

1428 Attempts by Jews to purchase the site of David's Tomb are resented by Christians. In retaliation, the Pope prohibits Italian ships from carrying Jewish passengers to the Holy Land.

Ottoman Period (1516–1917 AD)

1516 Sultan Selim I of Turkey captures Jerusalem, and the keys of the city are handed to him in Gaza.

1535 Suleiman I, the Magnificent, begins to rebuild Jerusalem's city walls and the Tower of David and to improve the water supply. The Sultan's Pool (used today to stage concerts and other entertainment) is named after him. He designates the Western Wall as the place of worship for the Jews. The first capitulation agreement is signed between Suleiman and King Francois I of France.

1541 The Golden Gate (also known as the Gate of Mercy) is sealed to prevent the entry of Jesus the Messiah, who, according to tradition, is expected to come through this gate. Sealing the gate is also attributed to security considerations.

1579 *Aliyah* continues as a group of 120 *olim* (immigrants) arrive from Damascus.

1622–1626
   Ibn Faruk's reign of terror against Christians and Jews.

1667 The arrival of false Messiah Shabtai Zvi, who was later excommunicated from the community.

1700 Judah the Pious and his community of 1,000 settle in the city and start building his famous synagogue.

1721 The synagogue is destroyed and for centuries left in ruins, hence the name *Hurva* (Ruins).

1737 The kabbalist Beit El Yeshiva is one of the 19 *yeshivot* (Jewish seminaries) founded in the 18th century.

1757 A Turkish decree re-establishes the status of the Greek Orthodox Church over the most important holy places.

1831 Mohammed Ali, Pasha of Egypt, rebels against the Sultan; his son Ibrahim captures Jerusalem and governs it for nine years, with a liberal approach toward Christians and Jews.

1834 Robert Curzon describes mass asphyxiation during a "sacred fire" ceremony at the Church of the Holy Sepulchre.

1840 End of liberal Egyptian rule. Alarmed by the Damascus blood libel, Sarajevo-born Rabbi Judah Alkalai urges Jews to settle in Jerusalem.

1842 Michael Alexander Solomon becomes the first Jewish bishop in Jerusalem in 1,700 years as Christ Church is founded.

1854 A dispute between Russia and France over the holy sites in Jerusalem and Bethlehem sparks the Crimean War. Canadian preacher, Henry W. Monk, settles in Jerusalem and petitions Queen Victoria to restore the city as the capital of a Jewish state.

1873 The ultra-orthodox religious neighborhood of Mea She'arim (100 Gates) is built. The German Colony is founded by the Templars.

1874 American Consul de Haas reports Jerusalem's population as numbering 30,000, of whom 20,000 (or two thirds) are Jews.

1878 The Congress of Berlin reaffirms the status of the holy places in order to prevent strife between Christian religious sects.

1882 The first secular school is opened by French Jewish organization, Alliance Israelite Universelle.

1883 General Gordon (a.k.a. Gordon of Khartoum) identifies Golgotha (Skull Hill) at Jeremiah's Grotto as the site of the crucifixion.

1890 A visit to Jerusalem inspires Swedish authoress, Selma Lagerloef, to write her book Jerusalem, for which she was awarded the Nobel Prize in 1909.

1896 The discovery of the Geniza manuscripts in Cairo sheds new light on the Jewish community in the early Islamic period.

1899 Joseph Rabinowitz, the Theodore Herzl of Messianic Judaism, becomes a believer after Messiah Yeshua reveals Himself to him on the Mount of Olives in Jerusalem.

1909 The establishment of Hachsharat Ha'yishuv is decided on at the 8th Zionist Congress. The company, headed by Otto Warburg, was instrumental in land acquisition, thereby furthering the urban development of Jerusalem.

1910 The German Augusta Victoria Hospital and Hostel is opened on Mount Scopus.

1911 Baedeker's guide reports Jerusalem's total population as 70,000, composed of 45,000 Jews, 15,000 Christians and 10,000 Muslims.

1914 Henry Morgenthau, US Ambassador to Turkey, organizes American aid totalling one million dollars for the Jewish community, cut off from its normal supply routes by World War I.

• The first aerial photographs of Jerusalem are taken by German World War I pilots followed by British and Australian pilots.

British Mandate Period (1917–1948 AD)

1917 Jerusalem surrenders to General Allenby. The British troops include volunteers of the Jewish Legion, and the Light Horsemen from Australia help to liberate Jerusalem.

1919 Sir Ronald Storrs, Governor of Jerusalem, begins restoration of Jerusalem's city walls. His decree that all buildings in the city must have a facade of Jerusalem stone is still in force today.

1920 Jewish defenders halt the first anti-Jewish riots during Passover. Their commander, Zionist Ze'ev Jabotinsky, is jailed by British authorities.

1922 Haj Amin ei-Husseini is appointed Mufti of Jerusalem and becomes the leader of the Arab insurgent movement.

1925 The Hebrew University on Mount Scopus is inaugurated by Lord Balfour, and Kibbutz Ramat Rachel is founded.

• Judah Leon Magnes, American rabbi and Jewish leader, settles in Jerusalem to become Chancellor and, later on, President of the Hebrew University. His advocacy of a bi-national state was both opposed by the Jews and not accepted by the Arabs.

1927 Jerusalem is shaken by an earthquake.

1929 The continued harassment of people praying at the Western Wall (e.g. removing the cloth screen dividing the male and female enclosures on *Yom Kippur*) causes indignation among world Jewry. Muslim agitation leads to countrywide riots, culminating in the killing of the Hebron and Safed Jewish communities.

1930 A British inquiry commission declares Muslim ownership of the Western Wall but confirms the Jewish right to worship. The ban on blowing the *shofar* (ram's horn) and other restrictions are not lifted.

1933 Arab Christian prophets in Jordan foresee that the nation of Israel will be reborn soon and begin prophesying about the natural restoration and spiritual revival of Israel and Jerusalem, the city of the Great King Yeshua.

1936 The establishment of the Arab Higher Committee under the Mufti of Jerusalem leads to increased disturbances and a general strike. The Royal Commission investigating the disturbances, headed by Lord Peel, recommends the partition of Palestine. The ensuing Arab revolt results in a high death toll among Jews, Arab rioters and moderate Arabs killed by Arab extremists.

• Haile Selassie, deposed Emperor of Ethiopia, finds refuge in Jerusalem.

1947–1948

By the end of the British Mandate, Arabs begin an attack against Jews. The Jordanian Arab Legion, commanded by British officers and helped by Egyptian semi-regular forces, shell Jerusalem. The 3-month siege ends with the opening of the Burma Road bypass. The Arab states, including Jordan, reject a UN plan to internationalize Jerusalem.

Israeli Period (1948 AD–Messiah Comes)

1948 After the War of Independence, Jerusalem is divided. East Jerusalem and the Old City remain in Jordanian hands, with the Jewish Quarter and its 58 synagogues destroyed and its Jewish population expelled. Israel retains West Jerusalem. Passage between the two parts is possible only through the Mandelbaum Gate. Prime Minister David Ben Gurion declares the State of Israel with Jerusalem as its capital.

1949 Israel and Jordan sign an armistice agreement. Despite UN supervision, Jordan violates it, denying Jewish access to the Western Wall, the Hebrew University campus and Hadassah Hospital on Mount Scopus and to the Mount of Olives Cemetery.

• Chaim Weizmann is elected the first President of Israel in a special session of the first Knesset.

• New Kiryat Yovel Quarter absorbs refugees from Arab countries.

1951 King Abdullah of Jordan, grandfather of King Hussein, is assassinated on the Temple Mount by Arab extremists. The Zionist Congress (the 23rd) is held in Jerusalem for the first time.

1953 *Yad Vashem* (Jerusalem's Holocaust Museum) opens on Memorial Hill in memory of the six million victims of the Holocaust. It is also a research and document center.

1961 Adolf Eichmann, the Nazi war criminal who perpetrated the Holocaust, is tried in Jerusalem, found guilty and hanged: the only death sentence ever carried out in Israel.

1964 Pope Paul VI visits Jerusalem and said, "Jerusalem represents the earthly point where God came into contact with man and where eternity crossed history."

1967 The Six Day War erupts. King Hussein orders his army to attack West Jerusalem despite Israeli warnings. In the ensuing battle, East Jerusalem falls into Israeli hands and the divided city is reunited. The Law for the Protection of the Holy Places is passed by the Knesset.

•Since this time, the spiritual restoration of Jerusalem has also begun (Luke 21:24-32). As of 2000 AD, over 300,000 Jews worldwide have received Messiah.

1977 President Anwar Sadat of Egypt comes to Jerusalem and addresses the Knesset, paving the way for the Camp David peace accords to be signed and for ties to be forged between Egypt and Israel.

1980 A special law is enacted by the Knesset re-affirming that united Jerusalem is the capital of Israel. Most foreign embassies in the city subsequently move to Tel Aviv. The International Christian Embassy Jerusalem is established.

• Crown Prince Fahd of Saudi Arabia declares a *jihad* (holy war) "to protect *Al Quds* (the Holy City) against Zionist aggression."

1987 Jerusalem House of Prayer for All Nations is established on the Mount of Olives.

1990 The US Senate and House of Representatives pass a resolution confirming that Jerusalem is the capital of Israel.

• The dispute over the St. John's Hospice in the Old City Christian Quarter in April and riots on Temple Mount in October, re-focus world public attention on the Jerusalem issue.

1991 At the Madrid Peace Conference, the Arab delegates reiterate their position that Jerusalem is to be the capital of the proposed Palestinian state.

• During the Gulf War, 39 missiles are fired at Israel from Iraq, but God protects Jerusalem (Psa. 121:4).

1993 The Oslo peace accord is signed in Washington, DC, in September between Prime Minister Yitzhak Rabin of Israel (who was assassinated a few years later) and Chairman Yasser Arafat of the Palestinian Authority, and facilitated by Bill Clinton, President of the United States. This brings a temporary end to the *intifada* (uprising) of the Arabs in Jerusalem and Israel.

1994 Jordanian King Hussein and Israeli Prime Minister Yitzhak Rabin sign a peace agreement.

1996 The 3000th anniversary of King David is celebrated in Jerusalem and around the world. At the same time, in a fuller way spiritually, God starts to restore the heart of David to His people worldwide.

2000 January 1 begins the year of transition from the second to the third millennia AD, based on the birth of Jesus the Messiah in Bethlehem. By this time, over two billion people worldwide believe that Jesus is Messiah, including over 300,000 Jews.

2000   Pope John Paul II visits Jerusalem in March and stays on the Mount of Olives. The Catholic Church, with its 900 million adherents, asks forgiveness of the Jewish people at *Yad Vashem* (Holocaust Museum). The Pope's visit motivated more improvements to Jerusalem, especially East Jerusalem, than any other event in the 20th century.

2000   *Rosh Hashana* (Traditional Jewish New Year) begins on September 29. The peace process initiated seven years prior, collapses over the status of Jerusalem.

   • More than 2,000 delegates from over 200 nations and Israel convene at the 4th All Nations Convocation Jerusalem to worship the King of Jerusalem and pray for God's true peace through Messiah.

   • National delegates from the nations, representing over two billion Christians worldwide, present a Scroll of Repentance to the Jewish people at *Yad Vashem* (Holocaust Museum), repenting for the Holocaust, anti-Semitism and replacement theology. The scroll was received on behalf of the Jewish people by Chairman Weiss, President of *Yad Vashem* and former speaker of the Knesset.

   • Delegates repent toward the Arab people for Christians' rejection of them, blessed them with a special offering from all nations, and welcomed them back into the household of faith in Messiah.

20??   When will Messiah be released from heaven by God the Father, to break the eastern sky, rend the heavens and come down? When will the fullness of Jerusalem's salvation be released to shine as a blazing torch? When will He put His feet on the Mount of Olives and take up the throne of David reigning as King of the Jews, Arabs and all nations? When will He bring about the ultimate peace we are praying for in Jerusalem and the whole world?

The fig tree (Israel) and all the trees (the nations) are blossoming. The Kingdom of God is near and Jesus is coming soon. Jesus said that this generation would not pass before His coming.

Chapter 5

Father Abraham's Vision

"Look to the rock from which you were cut and to the quarry from which you were hewn; look to Abraham, your father, and to Sarah, who gave you birth. When I called him he was but one, and I blessed him and made him many. The LORD will surely comfort Zion and will look with compassion on all her ruins; he will make her deserts like Eden, her wastelands like the garden of the LORD. Joy and gladness will be found in her, thanksgiving and the sound of singing" (Isaiah 51:1b-3).

Abraham is the father of us all. All Jews and Arabs are his children in the natural, and all believers are the children of Abraham in the spirit by faith in Jesus Christ (Gal. 3:7).

Adam had been created without sin, but he rebelled against God and was removed from the presence of God. The human race continued in selfishness and iniquity until God decided to wipe out the known world. Noah and his family were saved from 40 days and 40 nights of endless rain that covered the whole earth and destroyed every living thing, because God told them to build an ark. Jewish oral tradition says that the ark was built at the port city now known as Jaffa–Tel Aviv, which would have been in the center of the Garden of Eden, which included modern Egypt–Israel–Assyria and Mount Ararat. After Noah had landed on Mount Ararat, in what was to become Assyria, God had to begin all over again. But man continued to sin, and God scattered mankind all over the earth.

Finally, God raised up Abraham, a man now known for his remarkable faith, and led him out of Ur.

"I will make you into a great nation and I will bless you; I will make your name great, and you will be a blessing. I will bless those who bless you and whoever curses you I will curse; and all peoples on earth will be blessed through you" (Genesis 12:2-3).

Building and Rebuilding Altars— Possessing the Land for God

Abraham built altars to possess the land for God and to remember when and where God spoke to him. Building altars was a common practice throughout Old Testament times. It was a way of marking the intervention of God in the lives of men in a tangible and enduring way. The rocks remained as a visible sign that God was faithful and true to His promises. Abraham built an altar in Shechem, where God first promised him the land as an inheritance. He also built an altar at Beth El, which God inspired Jacob to call the Gate to Heaven, as he entered the Promised Land from the north. God then took him to Egypt for a time, before he was allowed to come back to build altars in Hebron and Jerusalem.

It is possible to say that Abraham relaid the foundations for God's ultimate purposes for the restoration of Jerusalem as he built an altar there; broke bread and drank wine with Melchizedek; made an oath to be loyal to the One God; and offered Isaac as a sacrifice. But God knew that a greater One, Jesus, was needed as the only truly significant and ultimate sacrifice. Instead of accepting the sacrifice of Isaac, God provided a ram—a substitute—until the appointed time. Today, God is calling us to rebuild the altars of prayer that Abraham built and to rededicate ourselves to God (Isa. 19: 19-21; Gen. 12:6-9, 13:3). This restoration through Yeshua will redeem the Fall of man in the Garden of Eden. (See map 2, page 188.)

Digging and Redigging Wells of Revival

Water is scarce in the Middle East, and wells, the source of water, are extremely important. Shepherds make sure that their flocks never stray too far from water, and caravans of old planned their trips according to the available water sources, the wells, along their way. To believers, wells represent the renewing work of the Holy Spirit. We are living in the days of restoration, when the emphasis of the Holy Spirit is on redigging the ancient wells, seeking the source of our life and our truth. Just as the deer pants after the water, so we are to pursue the Living Waters of God. As we learn about the ancient wells, we come to an understanding of how God can work in our lives during this time in history.

The first well mentioned in the Bible is in Genesis 16:13-14, where Hagar said, "**I have now seen the One who sees me**"—for this reason the well was called *Beer Lahai Roi* (the well of the one who sees Me and lives). Hagar bore Abraham a son and Abraham gave him the name Ishmael. Isaac was coming from *Beer Lahai Roi* when he met Rebecca and then lived there in *Beer Lahai Roi* even after Abraham's death (Gen. 24:62, 25:10-11). The two sons of Abraham, therefore, are linked to each other through the first reference to a well in the Bible. This is the most ancient well that can be re-opened.

As Isaac and Ishmael were linked to this well in the natural, the Lord wants them to be reborn out of the same spiritual well today. God revealed Himself to Hagar as the One who watches. God is still watching this ancient well to see His purposes for the salvation of the children of Isaac and Ishmael to be reconciled in Messiah accomplished. God is speaking to both the sons of Ishmael and Isaac, telling them, "**With joy shall you draw water from the wells of salvation**" (Isaiah 12:3).

In Genesis 21:30-34, Abraham dug a well and the place was then called Beersheva and "**there he called upon the name of the Lord, the Eternal God.**" Abraham, more than anyone else, saw things on earth from an eternal perspective. God is now speaking worldwide about redigging the old wells of revival and restoring the foundations of faith in preparation for the new Jerusalem.

Temporal or Eternal Vision

Abraham was a true visionary, a man of faith, who believed the Lord and the Lord credited it to him for righteousness:

> "**By faith Abraham, when called to go to a place he would later receive as his inheritance, obeyed and went, even though he did not know where he was going. By faith he made his home in**

> the promised land like a stranger in a foreign country; he lived in tents, as did Isaac and Jacob, who were heirs with him of the same promise. For he was looking forward to the city with foundations, whose architect and builder is God" (Hebrews 11:8-10).

Abraham was God's man, probably as much as anyone else other than Jesus. He was able to see things from God's eternal perspective. Abraham saw the day of the Lord and envisioned a new Jerusalem 4,000 to 5,000 years before it was to come down from heaven.

> "By faith Abraham, when God tested him, offered Isaac as a sacrifice. He who had received a promise was about to sacrifice his one and only son, even though God had said, 'It is through Isaac that your offspring will be reckoned.' Abraham reasoned that God could raise the dead, and figuratively speaking, he did receive Isaac back from death" (Hebrews 11:17-19).

Abraham was a true sojourner. He was willing to go out, not knowing where he was going. He lived in tents and was not enthralled with the physical city of Jerusalem, being more of a wilderness dweller, although spiritually he was the founder of Jerusalem. He was not looking to build a tabernacle, temple or physical city.

Jesus said, "**Abraham rejoiced at the thought of seeing my day, he saw it and was glad**" (John 8:56). It seems he understood that Jesus would be the ultimate sacrifice and rise from the dead instead of Isaac. Abraham not only saw Jesus being sacrificed but he also saw "**a city with foundations whose author and builder was God.**" Abraham's vision was not to build his own kingdom, but the Kingdom of God. His vision, in many ways, cut right through all of the temporal tabernacles, temples, church buildings and denominational divisions of Judaism and Christianity. Abraham understood that all those spiritual things would be burned by fire in the end. Abraham's vision was much like that of Jesus, who said, "**Before Abraham was born, I am**" (John 8:58), and "**Abraham saw my day and was glad.**" One could say that Jesus was looking through Abraham's eyes, or that Abraham was looking through Jesus' eyes.

Abraham and Jesus had many things in common. They were both sojourners. Jesus, as a sojourner, said, **"Foxes have holes, and the birds of the air have nests, but the Son of Man has nowhere to lay his head" (Luke 9:58).** He also said that His kingdom was not of this world, reinforcing this message. Abraham lived in tents as well. Each of these men was not limited by what they saw around them in the temporal world. Both were focused on what was to come, on the ultimate purposes of God. They focused on the unseen. In their visions, neither gave any great significance to earthly structures of symbols of status or position. As shepherds, both of them cared deeply for those close to them.

Both Jesus and Abraham were looking for the new Jerusalem, coming down out of heaven from God, prepared as a Bride, beautifully dressed for her husband Jesus. The ultimate dwelling of God will be with men, in the city with the 12 gates, with 12 angels on the gates, and the names of the 12 tribes written on the gates. The wall has 12 foundations on which are written the names of the 12 apostles of the Lamb. The gates are each made of a single pearl, and the great street is made of pure gold like transparent glass. This city will never have to be repaired or rebuilt, as it is the Eternal City. Both the city and the people in it will never get old but will be eternally young.

The new Jerusalem will measure 2,200 square kilometers, and cover the approximate distance from the Nile to the Euphrates. The city wall will be 200 feet thick. The heavenly city contains elements of the physical Jerusalem, the Temple and the Garden of Eden. It will be the ultimate city, of which the others preceding it were merely shadows. The greatest thing about the Holy City is that the Lord God Almighty and the Lamb are its temple. The Glory of the Lord gives it its light, and the Lamb is its lamp. The glory and honor of the nations will be brought into it. All those whose names are written in the Lamb's book of life, who are destined to be the Bride of the Lamb for eternity, will dwell within this city in perpetual joy and celebration.

God said to Abraham that his descendants would possess the gates of his enemies (Gen. 22:17). May the sons of Abraham possess, by faith, the gates of the nations and Jerusalem for the Kingdom of God leading to the new Jerusalem.

If the leaders of God's people today had Abraham's vision, think of how many billions of dollars and millions of laborers would be redirected from largely temporal visions to the eternal vision, purpose and destiny. May God deliver us from temporal, traditional, denominational and materialistic thinking; may He deliver us from all misdirected energies and labor in dead works so we may work towards His ultimate purposes.

Egypt—a Place of Prophetic Birthing

"Now there was famine in the land, and Abram went down to Egypt to live there for a while because the famine was severe" **(Genesis 12:10).**

Egypt (or the area of what became Egypt) is a place of prophetic birthing. It is a likely source of where Adam began the first civilization in history before the Flood. As Egypt is generally mentioned first in the Bible and as it is fair to assume that Adam was the father of a civilization, it is possible that Adam was the father of this people in the area of what, after the Flood, became known as Egypt. After the Fall of Adam and the Flood, Noah landed in Assyria, in the area of Mount Ararat. Abraham later came from this region looking for the city with foundations, whose builder and maker is God.

Father Abraham entered the Promised Land from Assyria and built his first altar at Shechem, where God first promised to give the land to his offspring. His second altar was built at Beth El, which became known as the gate to heaven. After this, Abraham went to Egypt.

After coming out of Egypt, he built the altars in Hebron and Jerusalem. Hebron is the place where both Ishmael and Isaac were born. The vision and first promises of the Promised Land were given in Shechem, but Abraham had to go to Egypt first before he could build the altars in Hebron and Jerusalem.

Soon after Abraham returned from Egypt, Ishmael was born. Abraham shared bread and wine with Melchizedek, possibly connecting the heir of God's promises to the last Adam, Jesus, the Righteous King. The altars at Shechem and Beth El were altars of promise. The altars built after Abraham's visit to Egypt were built in Hebron and Jerusalem to seal the covenant with God and were the first-fruits of the ultimate fulfillment of the promises.

It is interesting to note that Ishmael's mother and wife were Egyptians, but that the promised seed could not come through Ishmael. Because of the failure of the first Adam, redemption could not come through the oldest son, who is connected with Egypt. Instead, God raised up Isaac, the younger son of Abraham, through whom His covenant of redemption came. Later, the children of Israel were also called out of Egypt into the Promised Land.

Similarly, Jesus went to Egypt with His parents shortly after His birth. In this way, He may have identified with the first Adam. If Adam birthed the first civilization before the Flood, a possibility is that the ark left the area of what is today Egypt and landed in Assyria (Mount Ararat). The ark is coming from the Egypt area, over the Israel of today and then to Assyria! Jesus later came to Jerusalem to die and be resurrected as the last Adam, the One who overcame death and the grave, who will be crowned as the King of Jerusalem. The first Adam failed, but Jesus, the last Adam, triumphed victoriously over death.

Seeing so many things birthed out of Egypt, it became apparent to me that there is a very strong prophetic significance to Egypt in the Scriptures as well as a strong counter-attack of demonic resistance forces coming to and from Egypt against God's redemptive purpose of Egypt, Israel and Assyria being a blessing in the midst of the earth. Possibly the first river of the Garden of Eden was in Egypt. The Pishon, the first river, flows through Havilah, a name for Egypt, and the Gihon, a second river, flows through Cush, known today as Ethiopia and Sudan.

I believe one of Egypt's historic and redemptive gifts is to be a place of prophetic birthing, which is confirmed in many ways in these last days. Here are ten ways in which Satan is trying to counterfeit God's purposes to use Egypt as a place of prophetic birthing:

1. Pharaoh tried to stop God's redemptive biblical purpose and at that time and until today we can also see how the enemy has been trying to stop God's purposes in the Egyptian and modern-day Exodus by trying to stop the Jews from leaving Egypt and all nations to come to Israel.

2. The worship of thousands of false gods of Egypt defying the true God of Israel.

3. It is believed that Freemasonry was begun first in Egypt and has brought about great deception and spread Babylonian influence throughout the world!

4. Herod tried to kill Jesus, stopping Him from going to Egypt and coming back to die for us as the ultimate sacrificial Lamb, as foreshadowed in Egypt.

5. Egypt was a Christian nation until the 8th century AD. Thereafter Islam destroyed many Christians. Muslims tried to replace God's purposes and imposed Islam on the nation, trying to stop the fulfillment of Isaiah 19:23-25. Today the largest training center for Muslim leaders in the world is in Cairo.

6. After Gandhi died and was cremated, his ashes were thrown into the Nile River, in the belief that along its banks was the first civilization.

7. In 1967, Anwar Sadat led Arab nations against Israel and Jerusalem. President Nasser of Egypt tried to destroy Israel in the 1950s and 1960s.

8. The Pharaoh spirit of control tries to affect the Church in Egypt and all nations in trying to hold back the purpose of God and stop the Joshua Generation from coming forth.

9. In September 1994, just a few days before we held the first All Nations Convocation Jerusalem, the United Nations held a world gathering in Egypt and projected a New Age agenda and a New World Order over the world.

10. At the turn of the century into the year 2000 AD, there was a very large New Age world gathering in Egypt at the pyramids trying to project the Pharaoh spirit of control and the New Age spirit over the world.

I humbly share the following 12 events, giving all glory to God, who, in a positive way, is continuing to birth things prophetically from Egypt:

1. In 1985, I led a prayer team to Egypt. Forty people worshiped the Lord together. The Holy Spirit fell in power, prophetic words came forth and we were on our knees before God. The Lord led us into prophetic prayer missions. We went to Mount Sinai, where Moses was first given the vision of leading the Israelites out of Egypt, and we blew a ram's horn to the four points of the compass, calling home the Jews from the four corners of the earth. As we made our way to the Red Sea, God told us that we were reliving the exodus from Egypt. He told me to take 40 people to Russia the following year to prepare for the exodus from the North. In Moscow, we did a Jericho March around the Kremlin. One week later the Communists agreed to release 12,000 Jews. It was the beginning of the Russian *aliyah* of over one million Jews since that time.

2. In 1991, the Lord called us to do a Jericho March around the Middle East, from the Nile to the Euphrates and to build altars in 12 locations. We began and ended in Egypt, praying for the Jews and Arabs to come to salvation and be reconciled to the Lord. We also prayed for this region to be restored as a blessing in the midst of the earth according to Isaiah 19:23-25. We know that Jesus will reign over all and make this region of Egypt–Israel–Assyria a blessing in the midst of the earth.

3. In 1992, we went to Tiberias. The Lord told us to go up from Metullah to Shechem, Beth El, Jerusalem and Hebron and build altars where Abraham had built altars. We then went to Egypt and did a Jericho March around the country's largest mosque, where 70 percent of all Muslim clerics in the world are trained.

4. In January 1993, we had our first All Middle East Convocation in Cairo, Egypt. Thirty pastors from Israel and seventy from Egypt worshiped the Lord together in Hebrew, Arabic and English. Messianic and Arab pastors led prayer and worshiped together. This was the first of ten planned Middle East convocations. There have been six

in Cyprus, one in Antioch and one in Amman. The tenth convocation was again held in Egypt in March 2000. They are part of Messiah's plan for peace in the Middle East.

5.   The Lord sent us to Cairo, Mecca and Medina. We did a Jericho March around Mecca and prayed for the salvation of the Muslims worldwide.

6.   In 1994, while speaking at a pastor's conference in Cairo, we realized that all of the members of the board of our All Nations Convocation team were in the same place, so we held our first committee meeting. It is fair to say that the All Nations Convocations were born in Egypt. I also met my Israeli travel agent who helps with our convocations at the Cairo airport in Egypt.

7.   Before a 1995 Christian conference in Iraq, the Lord showed me that I needed to go to Egypt first, then to Iraq. An Ethiopian pastor, from the source of the Nile, was traveling with me. The Egyptian president had just escaped assassination in Ethiopia, so the officials did not want to let the Ethiopian into Egypt. We traveled from Egypt to Israel to Iraq and to Assyria, praying for these places, and sharing the message of salvation with the people we met. God showed us that Abraham walked this highway from Egypt through Israel to Assyria.

8.   Some 700 Christian leaders attended our 1996 national pastors' conference at the Gihon Hotel in Addis Ababa, Ethiopia. We were the first people from Israel to preach from the pulpits of Ethiopia. There was a significant breakthrough of repentance as leaders wept and renounced anti-Semitism. The people had not accepted the Jews in their midst, but now began to open up to them.

9.   In 1997, 42 African nations were represented at a conference we held at the facility of the Organization of African Unity, again in Ethiopia. Intercessors were seated in the very seats of the OAU representatives and African heads of state, rescinding racism and anti-Semitism, and praying for the salvation of the African continent, in particular for the leaders. Now, revival is increasing in Africa, and there are numerous believing heads of state. Benin is the first African nation trying to move its embassy to Jerusalem.

10.   In 1998, my book, *The Watchmen,* was dedicated in Uganda, at the source of the Nile River at a conference with John Mulinde. Numerous people who wrote recommendations happened to be there.

11.   In 1999, I delivered a message on the highway from Egypt through Israel to Assyria from Uganda, in which is the source of the Nile. Later an Egyptian who attended our Watchman's School of Ministry joined our staff at Jerusalem House of Prayer for All Nations.

12.   In 2000, our 10th All Middle East Convocation was held in Egypt and we sensed our first major breakthrough and release. Also in the year 2000, God promised me an apartment in Caesarea, Israel. Caesarea is the gateway to the nations and where the Gentiles first received the Holy Spirit. Today two billion people profess faith in Jesus. It is also the place from which Paul sailed to Rome. Today Caesarea represents the restoration of the Holy Spirit and the fire and Gospel coming full circle from the Gentiles at the ends of the earth back to Jews in Israel and Jerusalem. The apartment was sold to me by a Jew from Cairo, Egypt, now living in Israel. My Jewish travel agent, whom I met in Cairo, Egypt, told me of the place.

I only mention the above points as a modern-day confirmation that not only throughout history, but also today Egypt is a place of prophetic birthing.

In the midst of many shakings, we need to pray for a full spiritual breakthrough from Africa-Egypt to Jerusalem, preparing the way for a full breakthrough peace coming to Jerusalem. Even as the first peace agreement in the natural came from Egypt with Anwar Sadat and Menachem Begin's agreement, so it probably will be spiritually as Isaiah 19:23-25 speaks about a highway beginning from Egypt and going to Israel and Assyria worshiping God as a blessing in the midst of the earth.

Pray for God to move from first-fruits to fullness for His prophetic purposes to be birthed from Egypt–Israel–Assyria, that this region will fulfill its prophetic redemptive gift purpose to be a blessing in the midst of the earth. In doing so you are fulfilling the prophetic mandate to pray for the peace of Jerusalem.

From Two Trees in the Garden of Eden to One Tree in the New Jerusalem

When some people read a book, they like to read the first and last chapters before they delve into the substance of the book itself. They want to get an idea of the plot and the characters, and they want to know how the story will end. If they like the ending, they will usually read the whole book.

It is no wonder that the Bible is the number one best-seller of all time, for it sets a timeless pattern for classical literary masterpieces, involving the reader from the first paragraph until the end. Genesis contains the great exposition of history, introducing us to numerous unforgettable characters and identifying the heroes and villains. Revelation tells us who wins. We also find ourselves becoming major characters in God's development of history as the narrative draws us out of passivity.

In the first chapter of Genesis, God creates the heavens, the earth and all living things. At this point the heavens and earth were united as one (before the Fall of mankind). It was heaven on earth, primarily because of God's manifest presence. In the second chapter, the writer gives us more information about the Garden of Eden—home to the first-fruits of creation. The Garden of Eden must have been a beautiful place, for when God looked out on all His creation, Scripture tells us that He was pleased.

No one knows for sure where the Garden of Eden was located. In Iraq, I visited a professor of religion at the University of Babylon. Since the Tigris and the Euphrates, two of the rivers that formed the border of the Garden of Eden, are in Iraq, I asked him where he thought the Garden of Eden was. He replied that he did not know. Although we do not know for sure, the Bible does give us a few other clues. We know that the other two rivers were the Pishon and the Gihon. The Pishon flowed through the land of Havilah, which is a name for Egypt; and the Gihon flowed through Cush, the biblical name for Ethiopia and Sudan. It is conceivable that the Garden of Eden possibly stretched from the Nile to the Euphrates. The center of this huge garden would therefore be located where the city of Jerusalem is today. Since the Tree of Life and of the Tree of the Knowledge of Good and Evil were in the center of the Garden of Eden, it is possible that they were locade in what is today known as Jerusalem. (See map 1, page 186.)

The following two passages are interesting for their references to Egypt and the Promised Land. The Great City (Jerusalem) is also figuratively called Egypt and Sodom. The dimensions of the new Jerusalem (about 1,380 miles in length, breadth and height, according to Revelation 21:16) more or less fit the distance from the Nile to the Euphrates, or the area covering Egypt, Israel and Assyria. Could it be that the new Jerusalem will cover the entire area of the Middle East (Isaiah 19:23)? Will the coming down of the new Jerusalem out of heaven to earth be like the restoration of the Garden of Eden?

> "Now when they [the two witnesses] have finished their testimony, the beast that comes up from the Abyss will attack them, and overpower and kill them. Their bodies will lie in the street of the great city, which is figuratively called Sodom and Egypt, where also their Lord was crucified" (Revelation 11:7-8).

> "Lot looked up and saw that the whole plain of the Jordan was well watered, like the garden of the Lord, like the land of Egypt, toward Zoar. (This was before the Lord destroyed Sodom and Gomorrah.)" (Genesis 13:10)

In the context of this scripture, the gates of Zion include the whole area from the Nile to the Euphrates, as all the nations in this region may have been included in the Garden of Eden:

"He has set his foundation on the holy mountain; the LORD loves the gates of Zion more than all the dwellings of Jacob. Glorious things are said of you, O city of God: 'I will record Rahab [Egypt] and Babylon among those who acknowledge me—Philistia too, and Tyre, along with Cush—and will say, 'This one was born in Zion.'" Indeed, of Zion it will be said, "This one and that one were born in her, and the Most High himself will establish her.' The LORD will write in the register of the peoples: 'This one was born in Zion.' As they make music they will sing, 'All my fountains are in you'" (Psalm 87).

God seems to be saying that He wants to see all Jews and Arabs in the Middle East to be born out of the gates of Zion, the heavenly Jerusalem. We say with the Lord, "Glorious things are spoken of you, O city of God." We believe God for tens of millions of Arabs in the Middle East and millions of Jews to receive God in their lives from Rahab (Egypt) and Babylon (Iraq); among those who acknowledge Him will be Philistia (Palestinians), Tyre (Lebanon), and Cush (Sudan). Indeed of Zion it will be said, this one and that one were born in her. The Lord will write their names in the register of His peoples—their names will be written in the Lamb's book of life. This one and that one are born in Zion. As they make music they will sing, "All my springs of joy are in you!" All our fountains are in God. All our delights are in God. All things that refresh are found in God's river and will make glad the city of God. As you pray for salvation to come to these nations, you are praying for the peace of Jerusalem!

Although we are not sure exactly where the garden was located, the Bible does tell us what could be found there. In addition to an abundance of plants and animals of every kind and size, Genesis mentions two trees. The first was the Tree of the Knowledge of Good and Evil. The second was the Tree of Life. The Bible does not tell us exactly what kind of trees they were. It is possible, however, that both the Tree of the Knowledge of Good and Evil and the Tree of Life were olive trees, because there are many references to two olive trees throughout the Bible. This is the case not only in Genesis, but also in Zechariah, Romans and the final book Revelation.

The first Adam was proud and disobedient, loved his life and lost it. He partook of the Tree of the Knowledge of Good and Evil and blocked the way to the Tree of Life.

God made two trees. He could have made just one tree, the Tree of Life. But in His sovereignty, He made two trees and commanded man not to eat of the Tree of the Knowledge of Good and Evil. One might wonder why He did this, because our lives would have been a lot easier without a free will. Many of our problems come from having to make difficult choices. Our spirit wars against our flesh, and we find ourselves doing the very thing that we do not want to do. But God does not want us to function as robots in His kingdom. Instead, He wants us to serve Him as unique individuals who choose God with their own hearts, minds and souls. Not even the Fall of mankind moved God to remove from us our capacity of a free will. The book of Joshua reminds us to **"choose for yourselves this day whom you will serve" (Joshua 24:15)**. The choice to follow God is made when we commit ourselves to the Lord and every day after that as we choose to obey Him and remain in the center of His will for our lives.

We have been made in the likeness and image of God, with freedom to choose. We need to make the right choice—between His path and the decisions we want to make for ourselves. All of history is a dramatic display of the dynamic tension between man having chosen his will instead of the will of God. Ultimately, however, the will of God will prevail.

Adam and Eve had a choice. They could be dependent on God and choose His will and way by laying down their lives and wills, or they could choose their own. They could trust God's direction for their lives, or they could rely on their own understanding of a situation and choose what appeals to their eyes. We all have to make similar choices they had to make. We can choose to remain dependent on God, or we can choose to love our life and be our own boss. It is an issue all of us have to deal with on a daily basis. It includes our finances, our relationships, our use of time and even our choice of vocation.

When the serpent tempted Eve, he did not present her with a profound philosophical discussion but instead appealed to the most basic of her senses. Eve saw that the fruit was good to eat and could provide nourishment. It was a thing of great beauty and pleasant to the eyes. And finally, it was a tree that could make her wise. Each of these things seemed very good in the natural but were against God's way and purpose.

Many of the solutions to our problems present themselves in an equally deceptive manner, and many people follow the same path of reasoning as Eve did. The path of conventional wisdom causes us to ask, "Does it look good, feel good, taste good?" If we can answer "yes" to these questions, we feel we have a reasonably good chance of making a wise decision. However, conventional wisdom does not necessarily lead to Godly decisions. We need Godly wisdom to hear and obey the voice of God, which is peaceable, loving and pure because we often face that same choice as Adam and Eve did: to choose between eating from the Tree of the Knowledge of Good and Evil or obeying the will of God.

The last Adam humbled Himself, was obedient unto death, laid down His life and saved it for eternity. He restored the way to the Tree of Life and will be the King of the restored new Jerusalem, the Garden of Eden.

In the Garden of Gethsemane, Yeshua made the hardest choice of His whole life. Everything He had ever done had led Him up to the one moment when He was given the opportunity to choose the will of God the Father or choose His own way. Yeshua, with His free will, also knew that He could do His will or the Father's. That He well understood the implications of His choice is clear by the agony of His suffering. How must this brutal choice have looked to him? Gruesome. Think of all the pictures you have in your mind of a crucifixion, of mangled and tortured bodies.

How did it feel? It felt like hell itself. Full of fear and terror, Yeshua perspired blood as He anticipated the choices before Him.

Crucifixion was a common form of execution during Yeshua's lifetime. There was not a Jew alive who had not seen the tortured and pain-wracked bodies hanging on crosses in Jerusalem.

Conventional wisdom would dictate that the choice Yeshua made in the garden was ridiculous. However, He chose to lay down His life for all humanity. His choice to follow the will of God was the pivotal moment of all human history, for it was at that time that the possibility of reconciliation with the Creator was restored to man. The choices of our lives are not always easy, nor pleasant. We are taught to claim our rights—human rights, civil rights, the right to life, gay rights, abortion rights, religious rights. But a true disciple of Jesus Christ is a dead person. On Good Friday in the year 2000 in Moscow, Russia, I was meditating on the fact that I was crucified with Christ (Gal. 2:20). If this is true, I have no rights. I have given up all my rights and have none left. I am a dead person and my only right is to do the will of the Father. Everything else is wrong and is really partaking of the Tree of the Knowledge of Good and Evil. Dietrich Bonhoeffer said that if Christ calls a man, He bids him come and die. He died at age 39, a martyr trying to stop Hitler and his atrocities. May we choose God's will and life in these days, even if it costs us our earthly lives.

According to the book of Acts, the first believers, who were Jews, went out into the entire world to be witnesses to all the earth. Jesus said to His disciples that they would be His witnesses in Jerusalem, Judea, Samaria and to the ends of the earth after they received power on the Day of Pentecost (Acts 1:8). The Greek word for "witness" is *martyros*. In the early ages of the Church, so many witnesses of the Lord were martyred, that this Greek word came to be used to describe somebody that dies for his faith, hence the word martyr. May we be willing to lay down our lives daily and ultimately if required of us.

The natural tendency is to say that if something is easy, it must be good. But Jesus was not looking at the natural realm, but instead endured suffering for the joy that was set before Him. If we intimately know and love God and as His sheep know His voice, we are able to make the choice to follow the Lamb wherever He goes and to not love our lives unto death.

Satan tries to tempt us through the lust of the eyes, the lust of the flesh and the pride of life, just as he tempted Eve in these areas.

Interestingly, Jesus was tempted in the same areas when He was led into the wilderness by the Spirit. When He was asked by Satan to turn stones into bread, He was tempted with the lust of the flesh. It is interesting in regard to the second temptation that Satan took Jesus to the highest point of the Temple. Knowing that Jesus' destiny was to be the Chief Cornerstone of the spiritual temple and that God had already laid Him down (*Jeru*) out of heaven as the Chief Cornerstone, Satan, who because of his pride rebelled against God, was now trying to trick Jesus into also rejecting His destiny, by tempting Him in the area of pride. The third temptation to inherit the kingdoms of the world and to worship Satan was the lust of the eyes. Satan also promised eternal life to Eve when he tempted her in the Garden of Eden (Jerusalem). However, Jesus triumphed over these temptations when He died in Jerusalem, which is the reason why we triumph over Satan with the blood of the Lamb (we are dead to sin and to the lusts of the flesh), the word of our testimony (instead of accepting Satan's offer of the kingdoms of the world, we witness to all nations about Jesus) and that we do not love our lives unto death (to live is Christ and to die is gain). We will not worship Satan, but God, even if it costs us our lives, thus overcoming the temptation to love our lives more than we love the Master. Jesus made a way for us to overcome these temptations, so we can overcome and become citizens of the new Jerusalem.

Partaking of the Tree of Life means partaking of the Lord. In admitting our total dependency on God, we are submitting ourselves to His plan, His purposes and His ultimate destiny for humanity. If instead we choose to partake of the Tree of the Knowledge of Good and Evil, succumbing to the temptation to partake of what is appealing to the senses, to the rational mind and to our emotional needs, then we reject God and enslave ourselves to the law of sin and death. Just as Eve's choice in the Garden of Eden looked good and seemed to be good for her and Adam, so do many of our choices look good and seem to hold positive results for us. Just as Eve was led astray by trusting her natural reasoning, we too can be led astray in the same fashion. Secular humanism, which holds to the principle that man is inherently good and that he is capable of improving his own world if allowed to follow his own inclinations, is a deceptive stronghold on the hearts and minds of modern man. To the natural mind, without God, it seems preposterous to say that man is basically wicked and selfish. Humanists are in bondage to their philosophy just as the followers of false religions are enslaved to their cultic creeds. They refuse to walk in the way of the Tree of Life.

From Two Trees in Genesis to One Tree in Revelation

Genesis mentions two trees. But by the time we get to the end of the book of Revelation, only one tree remains. There are no accidents in the writing of the Bible; each named thing, whether person or object, has meaning. There has to be a reason for the one tree disappearing from the narrative.

At the beginning of time, in Genesis, mankind was given a lifetime to make choices. God commanded him not to eat of the Tree of the Knowledge of Good and Evil. He could choose to obey or disobey God. Later, we learn about the Tree of Life:

> "And the Lord God said: 'The man has now become like one of us, knowing good and evil. He must not be allowed to reach out his hand and take also from the tree of life and eat, and live forever'" (Genesis 3:22).

The first Adam was banished from the garden because of his choice to disobey God. He had to be removed from the Tree of Life. The only way to get access to the Tree of Life subsequent to Adam's fall, was through animal sacrifices, which pointed the way to Jesus' ultimate sacrifice. To accept Jesus' sacrifice, to obtain salvation and be able to partake of the Tree of Life, is the choice every man is confronted with today.

At the end of time, in Revelation, no choices will remain and man will reap the good or evil consequences of his choices because each person will have had the opportunity to choose his own way and cause. At the end of history, only those who have chosen the Tree of Life will remain to enter eternity in fellowship with the Father. The rest will be separated from God. There will no longer be the option to make personal choices. The one tree that will be left represents the Tree of Life or the choice for God.

Let us review the history of the two trees that, for us as believers in Yeshua our Messiah, represent the process of moving from first-fruits to fullness. The story of the two trees is the story of how those who choose life in Yeshua inherit the Tree of Life and of how God restores to His people the benefits of the Tree of Life, which is the tree chosen by the last Adam and all of His disciples.

Tree of Life

Tree of the Knowledge of Good and Evil

In the Garden of Eden, God placed two trees, the Tree of Life and the Tree of the Knowledge of Good and Evil (Gen. 2:9). Adam and Eve partook of the latter and had to leave God's presence in the garden.

Through Abraham, God initiated a new covenant. Abraham was justified by faith in a coming Messiah who would pay the penalty for sin with His own blood—even as the ram (lamb) was a substitute sacrifice for Isaac:

> "Abraham looked up and there in a thicket he saw a ram caught by its horns. He went over and took the ram and sacrificed it as a burnt offering instead of his son. So Abraham called that place The Lord Will Provide" (Genesis 22:13-14).

> "Then I saw a Lamb, looking as if it had been slain, standing in the center of the throne, encircled by the four living creatures and the elders" (Revelation 5:6a).

As part of the new covenant with Abraham, God made a way for His people to be part of a cultivated Tree of Life again. Man was restored to the relationship he enjoyed with God in the garden.

God promised to send the Messiah, the promised Seed, through Isaac. Although He promised to bless Ishmael (Gen. 21:12-13), Abraham's firstborn son rebelled against God's plan and against his father. He became a wild branch that had to be torn out of the cultivated tree of God's covenant.

When the promised Messiah came, His own people—the Jews—did not recognize Him. As a result of their unbelief these Jewish branches were broken off from their own cultivated olive tree (Rom. 11). Jesus wept over Jerusalem and said that His own people would not see Him again until they welcomed and acknowledged Him as their Messiah (Matt. 23: 37-39).

Although Jesus' own people rejected Him, a remnant of believers remained. As they started to spread the Gospel throughout the world, it ignited a flame among Gentiles who came to know Jesus as Savior. As they did, they were grafted into the cultivated olive tree of faith in Jesus as Messiah, but the majority of Jews remained broken off and detached from the True Vine. However, a few were grafted back into the olive tree. In these days of restoration, God is bringing the fullness of the Gentiles into the cultivated olive tree, but also grafting the natural branches, the believing Jews (Rom. 11).

Before Jesus entered into the world to shed His blood and prepare the way for the two to become one, there were two olive trees and *menorahs* of witnesses. One olive tree and *menorah* is the Jewish people, God's chosen people. The other is a picture of the Gentiles who will later be grafted into the cultivated olive tree.

Jesus is in the process of bringing the two into one cultivated olive tree. In Acts 2 Jesus said His people shall be His witnesses to Jerusalem, Judea and the ends of the earth. Revelation 11 talks about two witnesses, two olive trees and two *menorahs*. In the progression of restoration God is taking a people (the broken-off branches of the Jewish people) from the cultivated olive tree and the Gentiles coming from the wild olive tree who receive Messiah and grafting them into the cultivated olive tree. He will also take the lampstand that has been biblically called to be a light to the nations (Israel) and the lampstand that is called the Church and make them one. The two witnesses of the Lord throughout history, Israel and the Church, are in the process of becoming one *menorah* and one cultivated olive tree. Once this process is completed, the kingdoms of this world will become the kingdoms of our Lord and His Christ and He will reign forever

and ever.

Zechariah saw a vision of the future unity between the Gentile Church and Israel (Zech. 4)—redeemed and united as one new man in Messiah. He saw two trees standing next to a single *menorah* (lampstand), indicating

that the grafted branches and the restored natural branches will together carry the light of Messiah as a *menorah* to all nations. The redemptive purpose of Israel and the Church is to be a light to the nations (Isa. 42:6; Matt. 5:14). This is the essence of what it means for the two *menorahs* to become one. As the redemptive purposes of Israel and the Church are restored into

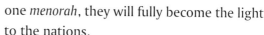

one *menorah*, they will fully become the light to the nations.

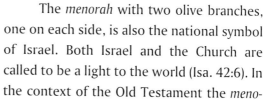

The *menorah* with two olive branches, one on each side, is also the national symbol of Israel. Both Israel and the Church are called to be a light to the world (Isa. 42:6). In the context of the Old Testament the *menorah* also refers to the seven spirits of God. Yeshua says, **"You are the light of the world, a city set on a hill that can not be hidden" (Matthew 5:14).** In Revelation we see Jesus walking in the midst of the seven lampstands, which are the seven churches. Jesus is both the King of Jerusalem and the Head of the Church. As branches from the Gentiles and branches from the

Tree of Life

Jews receive Yeshua, they come into the *menorah* and one olive tree. Together they can then become the light of the world.

The concept of the one new man is expounded in Romans 11:24, Revelation 11:3-4 and 22:1-2. Jesus is the True Vine. As Jewish and Gentile (including Arab) believers are grafted back into Messiah, they become in Yeshua like the Tree of Life to the world. Their fruit is available 12 months of the year and their leaves bring healing to the nations. The concept of the one new man is also explained in Ephesians 2 and Isaiah 19, where the children of Ishmael (Gentiles) and Isaac (Jews) are reconciled to become a blessing in the midst of the earth. Revelation 22:2 says the leaves of the tree (singular) will be for the healing of the nations.

The Tree of Life Represents the One New Man in Jesus

In Revelation 11:4, the two olive trees represent the cultivated olive tree of Romans 11:24, which is the Tree of Life. The two witnesses (Israel and the Church in Yeshua) represent the one new man of Jew and Gentile becoming one. This is happening today.

> "'And I will give power to my two witnesses [the one new man], and they will prophesy for 1,260 days, clothed in sackcloth.' These are the two olive trees and the two lampstands that stand before the Lord of the earth" (Revelation 11:3-4).

In the above passage, I believe both the two *menorahs* (lampstands) and the two olive trees could represent Israel and the Church. The reason for the separation is that the Jewish people (the natural branches) have still not fully entered into their rest as one new man in the promises of God by being grafted into the cultivated olive tree with the wild olive branches He has already grafted in. God had intended for His people to be the reflection of His heart. But when His people turned from Him, He allowed the Gentiles to receive the Gospel. This never meant that He had given up on His people, or that He intended for them to be separate from His Body.

The Bible talks about a future unity between the Church and the Jewish people:

> "He [the angel] asked me, 'What do you see?' I answered, 'I see a solid gold lampstand with a bowl at the top and seven lights on it, with seven channels to the lights. Also there are two olive trees by it, one on the right of the bowl and the other on its left'" (Zechariah 4:2-3).

Here we see the process of restoration moving forward. We see only one lampstand and two olive trees. It is interesting that today the *menorah* with seven candlesticks is the natural symbol of Israel, even while it also represents the Church at large and the seven churches of Revelation 1:20. The two olive trees represent Israel and the Gentile Church.

One could say that the one lampstand here represents the heavenly, eternal unity between the Church and Israel. In God's perspective, they are meant to be united. The fact that two trees remain indicates that the work is not yet completed.

> "After all, if you were cut out of an olive tree that is wild by nature, and contrary to nature were grafted into a cultivated olive tree, how much more readily will these, the natural branches, be grafted into their own olive tree!" (Romans 11:24)

Here, there is one cultivated olive tree, the one True Vine who is Yeshua and all else is grafted into Him (John 15). There is no mention of the *menorah*, because all differences will disappear in the unity of the cultivated olive tree. Jew and Gentile will fully become the one new man by the time of Messiah's return.

The believing Gentile branches are being cut out of the wild olive tree and being grafted into the cultivated olive tree with the natural Jewish branches, who are also being grafted back into their own olive tree. The cultivated olive tree, the Tree of Life, will replace the dead wild olive tree and its branches forever. We are progressing from two trees in Genesis to one tree in Revelation, where the leaves of the Tree of Life, which represents the entire community of the redeemed, will be for the healing of the nations:

> "Then the angel showed me the river of the water of life, as clear as crystal, flowing from the throne of God and of the Lamb down the middle of the great street of the city. On each side of the river stood the tree of life, bearing twelve crops of fruit, yielding its fruit every month. And the leaves of the tree are for the healing of the nations" (Revelation 22:1-2).

The connection between Eden, Jerusalem and the ultimate destiny of all creation is therefore inextricably linked to what happens in the restoration and joining of all things in heaven and earth in Messiah.

Let us now move through Genesis a little bit and get an idea of how the choices made by the two Adams regarding the two trees played themselves out in history. The first Adam, God's first creation, was in the Garden of Eden when he made his choice against God. As we said, the heart of Jerusalem could be the very center of the garden, which means that the Tree of the Knowledge of Good and Evil could have been located in what later came to be known as Gethsemane.

Jesus, the last Adam, was in the Garden of Eden (Gethsemane) when He chose to do the will of God the Father. His choice brought life to the world. In Genesis 15 we read of God's covenant with Abraham and the promise of the land from the Nile to the Euphrates. I believe God has promised all this land as a place for the Jews and Arabs (the sons of Isaac and Ishmael) to dwell together in unity. On the day when God made a covenant with Abraham, a smoking firepot with a blazing torch appeared and passed between the pieces. This may be a picture of the separation between Isaac and Ishmael that was about to come. Today, the God of restoration is again passing between Jews, Arabs and Gentiles with a smoking firepot and blazing torch, uniting and lighting them as one new man. Then He will make them a blessing in the midst of the earth.

Chapter 16 opens with the birth of Ishmael through an Egyptian handmaiden (Hagar). Ishmael, his firstborn and oldest son, is circumcised as a sign of the covenant in chapter 17. God also shows that Isaac will be born and an everlasting covenant—man's eternal covenant with God through His Son Jesus—will be established with Isaac.

In Genesis 16, we read the story of Ishmael and Isaac. Hagar had just been banished by Sarah. It was a very difficult moment for this young woman. Actually, she had submitted to her mistress Sarah when Sarah told Abraham to go in to her. It was the custom of those times for women who could not have children to use their maids as surrogates; the child born out of such a union would be traditionally raised as the son or daughter of the household.

After Hagar conceived, she was mistreated and fled into the wilderness. Can you imagine how she must have felt? Lonely, destitute and afraid. What does God tell her to do? To go back to the very mistress who mistreated her! He told her to submit to Sarah and He would give her a son.

Hagar went back and was ultimately welcomed in the community. But her son, Ishmael, did not submit. The Scriptures describe him as a wild man, constantly in conflict with his brothers. What happened to Ishmael? He was set apart, separated from Abraham and his descendants because of his rebellion.

Ishmael was a wild branch that was broken off. Had there not been this break, there could have been unity between the sons of Ishmael and the sons of Isaac. But in this case, the wild branch did not submit and was broken off. Ishmael's choice for himself still continues to change the course of history.

This is what is spoken about in Zechariah 4, when it talks of two olive trees. In this chapter, the question, "What does this mean?" is asked five times. First, the prophet talks about the two olive trees and then he talks about the branches. What are the trees and what are the branches? What does this mean?

In Romans 11, we read of the wild olive branches being cut off and we know that these were the Gentiles in general. Ishmael was a Gentile, in that he was not a Jew. He was a wild branch that was broken off, as he did not submit to his brother Isaac, the child that the promise of redemption would come through. This was the break between the sons of Abraham that has endured to this day and continues to impact the course of history.

Galatians 4:24 provides us with a picture of two covenants. The covenant given to Moses at Sinai—the law represented by Hagar the slave—makes slaves of us. The discussion of sonship and covenant in Galatians 4 echoes back to Genesis 21, quoting the words of Sarah, who said, **"Cast out that bondwoman and her son, for the son of the bondwoman shall not be heir with the son of the free woman."** Why? Because he, Ishmael, on the day that Isaac was weaned, mocked Isaac. And because he scorned his brother and refused to submit, he was cast out.

The children of such a covenant born out of rebellion are slaves to the law. If we look at the present city of Jerusalem, we realize that the city is in extreme bondage. One has only to walk around the city to see how deeply the people are enslaved. Orthodox Jews are slaves to the impossible rigors of their observances. Muslims are enslaved to Islam. The calls to prayer which echo throughout the city five times a day are a poignant reminder of the leash which binds these people. Many Christians are equally enslaved to religious spirits that create conflict and divisiveness where there need be none. In other words, all those who are not born again are slaves to sin.

Jesus is our life. The law of the spirit in Christ Jesus has set us free from the law of sin and death and has brought us into the new covenant. We can say that we have moved from Mount Sinai to Mount Zion, as God promised in Isaiah 28:17-18:

> **"See, I lay a stone in Zion, a tested stone, a precious cornerstone for a sure foundation; the one who trusts will never be dismayed. I will make justice the measuring line and righteousness the plumb line; hail will sweep away your refuge, the lie, and water will overflow your hiding place. Your covenant with death will be annulled; your agreement with the grave will not stand."**

In the Garden of Gethsemane, Jesus faced the ultimate choice: life or death. In the natural, the choice He made flew in the face of conventional wisdom that would have pointed towards self-protection and avoidance of suffering. Had He gone that way, however, the world would have remained in darkness and there would have been no hope of redemption. Instead, a choice that made no sense in the natural was the source of life for all of mankind. Jesus, as the last Adam, was redeeming the choice of the first Adam—possibly in the very place in Jerusalem where Adam made his choice against God.

Recently, I spent some time in the Garden of Gethsemane and was directed to look closely at one of the old olive trees. It was probably there in the time of Jesus as many of these trees are known to be 2,000 years old. It looked like one tree, but when I got closer to it, I could see that the trunk was cleft, making it look like two trees. The Lord said, "Look," and the truth of what I was seeing jumped out at me. I felt as if I were looking at a fulfillment of Romans 11, in which the two trees became one tree. Yeshua was the last Adam, and He chose to partake of the Tree of Life in the same garden whereas the first Adam chose to partake of the Tree of the Knowledge of Good and Evil.

Jesus said that the kingdom was taken from Israel and given to a nation that brings forth fruit. He is the Head of the Church, since His ascension into heaven. The natural branches were broken off and scattered. Jerusalem was destroyed in 70 AD, and the Jews were scattered throughout the whole earth. Israel as a nation ceased to exist and the body of believers in His Son became God's witness on earth.

The natural branches, the Jews, were cut off spiritually when they rejected Jesus, and the Jewish people then became a wandering people. Since they were no longer attached to the true vine, they grew wild and at random. Their history is a sad testimony to the consequences of their falling away. They have strayed from the true God and are flocking to embrace false gods. Young Israelis flock to Indian holy places in search of spiritual fulfillment. Israel is rife with a variety of faith healers, spiritualists and even Satanists, as God's own people seek after other gods. One can easily say that most of the Jews today are spiritually lost.

However, we who have read the last chapter, know that this is not the way God intends to end the story. Revelation 11:4 returns us to the two trees that we encountered in Zechariah 4. Now there are two olive trees. Here, we are specifically told that they are olive trees. There are also two lampstands.

At the beginning of Revelation, the Church is represented by two lampstands. We know from the Old Testament that the *menorah* (lampstand), which is also the symbol of Israel, represents the seven spirits of God. In the *menorah*, the Church and Israel are linked as one. At the end of Revelation 11, the trumpets blow and Messiah returns. The two trees are not mentioned again.

At that time, there will be one king, Yeshua. All that is separate, cast off and broken will become unified, for we know that Jesus Himself will bring about the restoration of all things. And in this ultimate restoration, the Church and Israel will become one. Romans 11 is a millennium chapter, for the unity it speaks of will come about only in the Messiah.

The cultivated olive tree in the book of Romans represents the Jew and the Gentile, united. The wild olive tree has been cast aside and we have one tree. Both stocks have merged into one tree. In Ephesians 2, Paul talks about one new man, which in fact speaks of the unity between Jews and Gentiles once they have been made one in Messiah. The wild olive tree is cast aside and the Gentiles become truly one in Messiah with the Jews. Both become part of the Israel of God (Rom. 11) and His one new man.

We are now living in the time of first-fruits of those promises and are seeing the fulfillment of the different pieces that will lead up to the ultimate restoration. When the fullness of the Gentiles comes in, all Israel will be saved. One has only to look at the vast numbers of people coming to faith in the Messiah throughout the world today to realize that the fulfillment of the time of the Gentiles is close.

Isaiah 19 presents us with another picture of the olive tree. Egypt, Assyria and Israel (Jew and Gentile, including the Arabs) will come together as one:

"In that day there will be an altar to the LORD in the heart of Egypt, and a monument to the LORD at its border. It will be a sign and witness to the LORD Almighty in the land of Egypt. ... In that day there will be a highway from Egypt to Assyria. The Assyrians will go to Egypt and the Egyptians to Assyria. The Egyptians and Assyrians will worship together. In that day Israel will be the third, along with Egypt and Assyria, a blessing on the earth. The Lord Almighty will bless them, saying, 'Blessed be Egypt my people, Assyria my handiwork, and Israel my inheritance'" (Isaiah 19:19-20,23-25).

In Genesis 17:19 God told Abraham that the promised covenant between Himself and the old patriarch would come through his son Isaac. It appears that Abraham thought that Ishmael would be the one the promised blessing would come through. Abraham, being concerned for his son Ishmael, asked God to also bless Ishmael, his first born, who was the first to be circumcised with Abraham. God agreed to bless the sons of Ishmael, promising to make them "a great nation." As much as God's promise for the Jews and the sons of Isaac as the chosen nation still stands, God's promise not to reject Ishmael but to make him a great nation also still stands. God could have said that He would make only Israel a blessing in the midst of the earth. Instead, he chose to call Egypt His own people and the Arab people of Assyria His own handiwork. He says together He will make them a blessing in the midst of the earth as one new man with Israel, His inheritance.

In these days God is not only reconciling Gentiles to Himself as the spiritual sons and daughters of Abraham by faith (Gal. 3:7), He is also reconciling the natural sons and daughters of Abraham—the Arabs and the Jews—into His everlasting covenant in Messiah. The reconciliation of Jews and Arabs is the first-fruits of the highway prophesied in Isaiah 19.

It is interesting that in Genesis 15, Abraham burned a heifer, goat and ram and cut the three animals in half, after which a firepot and torch appeared and passed between the pieces. Could this be a picture of Egypt, Israel and Assyria that were cut in half as the Jew and Gentile, or as Ishmael and Isaac were separated but are now being reconciled in the Messiah as one new man? The next chapter speaks of the birth of Ishmael and Isaac, and their covenant with God. In John 15, we have yet another picture of a tree. Yeshua describes Himself as the True Vine. He tells His disciples that, apart from Him, they can do nothing. At the end of Revelation, we are struck with the similarities between the Garden of Eden and the Holy City of Jerusalem. The first Adam was in Eden/paradise (possibly Jerusalem) when he disobeyed God. The last Adam was also in Jerusalem when He chose life. At the beginning of God's story of mankind, there were two trees in the Garden of Eden. At the end, in the book of Revelation, we are left with one tree.

Psalm 1 presents a compelling picture of the man or woman who partakes of this tree, telling us that he who meditates on God's Word day and night like a faithful watchman,

> **"He is like a tree planted by the streams of water, which yields its fruit in season and whose leaf does not wither. Whatever he does prospers" (Psalm 1:3).**

At the end of Revelation—the end of the story of God's involvement with mankind on earth and before His coming to unite all things in heaven and on earth—we read this wonderful promise for those who overcome and partake of the Tree of Life:

> **"He who has an ear, let him hear what the Spirit says to the churches. To him who overcomes I will give the right to eat from the tree of life, which is in the paradise of God" (Revelation 2:7).**

> **"The throne of God and of the Lamb will be in the city [the new Jerusalem] and his servants will serve him. They will see his face, and his name will be on their foreheads...." (Revelation 22:3-4).**

> **"Blessed are those who wash their robes, that they may have the right to the tree of life and may go through the gates into the city" (Revelation 22:14).**

Chapter 7

Removing the Ten Stones

> **"Pass through, pass through the gates! Prepare the way for the people. Build up, build up the highway! Remove the stones. Raise a banner for the nations"** (Isaiah 62:10).

In the following pages we will discuss ten stones that need to be removed for peace to come to Jerusalem. Jerusalem is represented by Jews, Arabs and others living within Jerusalem's Old City. It also represents all of Israel, because it is the capital of all the land. God, which is represented by Jerusalem in a broader and eternal sense, promised the land from the Nile to the Euphrates as these are the approximate dimensions of the new Jerusalem. So Jerusalem represents everything from the modern day Old City to the new Jerusalem coming down out of heaven. In these last days God is calling us to pray not just about the problems (although it is necessary and important to pray over problems and crises as they arise), but our primary focus should be to pray into the purposes of God. If we do this, many of the crises will take care of themselves. May God help us to be purpose-oriented in our prayers, and not just crisis-oriented.

Praying for these ten stones to be removed is a process. People have been praying in this way since 1996, and we have seen real progress in regard to the pushing back and at least partial removing of these stones. We need to continue praying for the fullness of the removal of these stones. This will help to prepare the way for the coming of Messiah.

Jesus must remain in heaven until the time of the restoration of all things (Acts 3:21). As we see these stones removed, which has to do with preparing the way for the people to come to salvation, reconciliation and restoration of God's purposes in Messiah, we will see the way prepared for Messiah:

"A voice of one calling: 'In the desert prepare the way for the
LORD; make straight in the wilderness a highway for our God.
Every valley shall be raised up, every mountain and hill made
low; the rough ground shall become level, the rugged places a
plain. And the glory of the LORD shall be revealed, and all mankind together will see it'" (Isaiah 40:3-5).

Use the information in these chapters for serious and travailing intercession so all Israel can be saved. In Psalm 122:6, God commands all believers
to pray for the peace of Jerusalem. We hope that you can stand from all
nations as God's watchmen and breakthrough warriors to see these stones
fully removed, preparing the way for the King.

Stone 1:
God's Peace Process vs. Man's Peace Plan

"Therefore hear the word of the LORD, you scoffers who rule
this people in Jerusalem. You boast, 'We have entered into a
covenant with death, with the grave we have made an agreement. When an overwhelming scourge sweeps by, it cannot
touch us, for we have made a lie our refuge and falsehood our
hiding place.'

So this is what the Sovereign LORD says:

'See, I lay a stone in Zion, a tested stone, a precious cornerstone for a sure foundation; the one who trusts will never be
dismayed. I will make justice the measuring line and righteousness the plumb line; hail will sweep away your refuge, the lie,
and water will overflow your hiding-place. Your covenant with
death will be annulled; your agreement with the grave will not
stand. When the overwhelming scourge sweeps by, you will be
beaten down by it'" (Isaiah 28:14-18).

"For to us a child is born, to us a son is given, and the government will be on his shoulders. And he will be called Wonderful
Counsellor, Mighty God, Everlasting Father, Prince of Peace. Of
the increase of his government and peace there will be no end.

He will reign on David's throne and over his kingdom, establishing and upholding it with justice and righteousness from that time on and forever. The zeal of the Lord almighty will accomplish this" (Isaiah 9:6-7).

Since we entered the 21st century, the newspapers worldwide have been full of stories about the Middle East peace process. The process leading up to peace, however, is anything but peaceful. Each step of the way is filled with argument and contention, with each side accusing the other of not abiding by the terms of the agreements. Still, negotiators meet around the clock at huge expense, hoping to take a few steps in the right direction.

Despite the good intentions of some politicians, as well as the honest desires of some Arabs and Jews to be able to live in peace and raise their families in safety, the current peace process can ultimately not succeed as long as it continues to exclude the Prince of Peace. It is a peace process that, no matter how humanly rational, reasonable and well motivated, will fail because it is built on human reasoning and not on the Word of God. Just as we discussed in chapter 6, the path of life often contradicts the rational and sane approach of human reasoning. In the case of the Middle East, any peace process which fails to take into account God's purposes for Israel, Egypt and Assyria is doomed to certain failure. Hong Kong is 20 times smaller than Israel and has six million people. There is room for all the Jews and Arab Palestinians in the world, in Jerusalem-Israel. Land-room is not the primary issue. Praying for the peace of Jerusalem means praying for the Arabs and Jews to fully realize the bankruptcy of and to abandon all options of false peace. The only hope is to make room in their hearts for the Prince of Peace, Messiah Yeshua, the King of Jerusalem, to reign. Only as Jews and Arabs receive Jesus today and prepare for His Second Coming, will lasting and perfect peace come to this region.

Yitzhak Rabin, a recent Prime Minister of Israel, was one of the nation's most honored and respected war heroes. He fought in all the major wars since and including the War of Independence. The son of Russian immigrants, he pledged his life to defend the Zionist dream as well as the physical boundaries of Israel. Eventually, he gave his life to this cause. Rabin was responsible for bringing the Israelis and the Palestinians to the negotiating table in what is now known as the Oslo accords, a carefully laid-out process intended to deal progressively with the differences between Israel and Palestine. The result hoped for was peace.

In the fall of 1994, Rabin was attending a rally for peace in Tel Aviv. He had just finished singing the words of a song of peace when he left the stage. The last thing he ever did was to fold the paper on which the words of the song of peace had been written and put it in his coat pocket. A few moments later, an assassin's bullet pierced the words of peace and killed the Prime Minister. Even in his death, the Prime Minister was unable to bring about peace, and conflicts continue to this day. When I heard of the assassination, I could not help but think of Isaac, the son of Abraham, because *Yitzhak* is the Hebrew name for Isaac. Had he been sacrificed, Isaac's death would not have brought peace either.

Jesus, the Messiah and Prince of Peace, is the only one who can bring about true peace in the Middle East. He died to bring forgiveness for our sins and break down the partition between Jew and Arab, as well as the barriers of prejudice and hate which separate people from all over the world. God has obviously allowed the present peace agreement between the Palestinians and Israel to continue. It does not mean that He is taking either side. When the Jewish people first entered the Promised Land after wandering in the desert for 40 years, Joshua asked the Lord, who had appeared to him as a man with a drawn sword, "**'Are you for us or for our enemies?' The Lord said, 'Neither'**" (Joshua 5:13-14). God was saying that He was not siding with the Jewish people or with the early inhabitants of Jericho, and I believe He is saying the same thing today. He is allowing the human peace process to develop at its own pace. At the right moment, He will intervene and will deal with the situation in his own way. When people finally realize that the man-made peace process cannot bring lasting peace, Arabs and Jews alike will turn to their Messiah.

If the Jewish people place their trust in a strong Zionist nation, they will not turn to the Lord. Similarly, if the Arab nations place their trust in a strong Islamic nation, they will not look to the true God. If politicians try to make peace by arbitrarily mixing Islam and Judaism together, expecting them to get along, then the peace process will be doomed to failure since, in the natural and without the sovereign intervention of the Holy Spirit, this is impossible. A Babylonian peace will eventually fall apart. There is no common denominator between Islam and Judaism.

We can go even farther. We can say that Muslims and Jews are sworn enemies of one another. Trying to unite the *Tanach* (Hebrew scriptures) and the Koran is like trying to mix oil and water. You can shake them up together, but they separate very quickly. The only true unity that is possible will come when Arabs and Jews embrace the truth of the Prince of Peace and the Word of God.

It is time for believers to step out into the forefront and to be bold about their faith. In the first century, 11 of the original 12 apostles were martyred, following the example of Messiah Jesus. If men like Yitzhak Rabin and Anwar Sadat could be assassinated in the name of man's peace process, as believers in the true God we have to realize that many among us may be martyred and killed as God's peace process emerges. The deaths of the saints will affect God's purposes and bring forth hundredfold fruit, for we know that "of the increase of his government and peace there will be no end." If Muslim and Jewish politicians are dying in the name of something that is not true, believers in the one God need to be able to follow the Lamb wherever He takes us and to "love not our lives even unto death" for the truth.

In the book of Revelation, the Lamb is mentioned 29 times, making the Lamb the major theme of this book. Jesus is the conquering Lamb. He also calls us to conquer as lambs. In the book of Romans, he says that we are as sheep sent to the slaughter. Yet in all these things we are more than conquerors. Jesus sends us out as lambs in the midst of wolves.

We need to pray for deliverance from the fear of death and ask for more boldness in our witness, standing on **Proverbs 28:1: "The wicked flee when no one pursues, but the righteous are as bold as a lion."** We need to be lambs with the boldness of lions. We also need to believe that the Lord will protect us as long as we are doing the things that He has called us to do. Until Jesus' hour had come, no harm could touch Him. If our hour has not yet come, God will surround us with angels to protect us. When our hour does come, we need to be able to say, along with the apostle Paul, **"For to me, to live is Christ and to die is gain" (Philippians 1:21).** If we are going to be effective in working out God's purposes, we need to overcome the fear of death and not run from our responsibilities, especially in difficult situations.

Martyrdom and persecution were seeds of revival in the first century and the Protestant Reformation, even in these last days all around the world. More people have been martyred in the 20th century than during the preceding 19 centuries put together, and it has been during the 20th century that we have seen the greatest revivals in history. Martyrdom and persecution will increase between now and the time when Jesus comes back, both in the nations and in Israel. This will release even greater boldness in proclaiming the Gospel, which will in turn lead to great revival and spiritual awakening around the world.

According to Revelation 6:10-12, this time of martyrdom will come before God's ultimate purposes are accomplished. This passage of scripture speaks of the full number of martyrs that has to be slain. Just as there have been many martyrs for Islam, man's Babylonian peace process and other false gods and ideologies, there surely will be many more martyrs for God's peace plan.

Scripture is clear on the events that need to take place before there is peace in Jerusalem. The return of the Jews from the four corners of the earth and true reconciliation between Arabs and Jews are like the two major pieces of the puzzle. These two keys to God's peace plan are the wings of the eagle! Even in the midst of the present day political turmoil, God's peace process is emerging as many people are coming to know Messiah, the Prince of Peace. We know that God's peace plan in Messiah will prevail and culminate in Messiah taking up the throne of King David in Jerusalem.

Pray for the peace of Jerusalem by praying for God's peace plan to replace man's peace process.

Stone 2:
The Salvation of the Arabs

The Arab peoples are the most friendly and hospitable people I have met anywhere in the world if they are accepted and loved. I have enjoyed living among them for over 13 years. When they accept and love Jesus as Saviour and Messiah, they will become a tremendous blessing in the midst of the earth. God will use the believing Arabs then to bring tens of millions of other Arabs to the Lord, provoking the Jews to jealousy. We need to pray as much for the salvation of the Arabs as for the Jews in these last days.

> **"In that day there will be a highway from Egypt to Assyria. The Assyrians will go to Egypt and the Egyptians to Assyria. The Egyptians and the Assyrians will worship together. In that day, Israel will be the third, along with Egypt and Assyria, a blessing on the earth. The LORD Almighty will bless them, saying, 'Blessed be Egypt my people, Assyria my handiwork, and Israel my inheritance'" (Isaiah 19:23-25).**

A Short History of Islam
—a Replacement Theology

After the death and resurrection of Jesus, the Gospel spread all over Israel, the Middle East, across Egypt, North Africa and into Assyria. We know that Christianity, brought by the Apostle Mark, had grown to be the faith of the majority of the people in Egypt and also through North Africa before the conquest of Islam. The Apostle Paul also established churches throughout what was then Assyria (today Asia Minor, Jordan, Turkey, Syria, Iraq and the Arabian peninsula).

In the 7th century AD, a young Arab named Mohammed, from the region which is now Saudi Arabia, received what he believed to be a revelation of the one true religion, and founded Islam. Growing up, Mohammed was exposed to a wide variety of religious traditions, including a form of corrupted Christianity and Judaism. Consequently his knowledge was faulty and based on incorrect teachings.

Originally, he instructed his followers to pray facing Jerusalem but, when he saw that the Jews were not embracing his new religion, he changed his orders instructing his followers to pray facing Mecca. Around the golden Dome of the Rock, situated on the Temple Mount in Jerusalem, are inscribed the words, "There is one God, his name is Allah and he has no son." Islam also teaches that God chose and made a covenant with Ishmael, not Isaac, and that Abraham took Ishmael to be offered on Mount Moriah. This immediately puts Islam at odds with the Christian faith and Judaism. Islam is the ultimate replacement theology. It teaches by word and implication that the Koran replaced the Bible; Mecca replaced Jerusalem; Ishmael replaced Isaac as the chosen son/seed; Islam replaced Judaism; the Muslim/Arab nations replaced Israel; the Mosque of Omar and the Dome of the Rock replaced the temple in the place where Jesus died; a mosque replaced the traditional site of Jesus' ascension. They claim all Jewish prophets were really replaced by Muslims from the beginning, including Jesus, and that Mohammed replaced Jesus as the greatest prophet.

The new replacement religion spread rapidly throughout the Middle East, including conquering Jerusalem/Israel as its possession and soon covered the whole area from Morocco to the borders of Iraq and Turkey. Islam eventually spread all the way across Asia to Indonesia, and today claims over one billion adherents worldwide.

From its beginnings, Islam has held to the concept of being one nation in the Middle East, not a series of independent and separate countries. During the early centuries of its history, the Islamic nation was ruled from Saudi Arabia and Syria, then for 500 years from what is today Iraq. For 400 years, the Arab nations were ruled by Turkey and was known as the Ottoman Empire. During the Gulf War of 1991, Saddam Hussein's goal was for the Arab states to be one Islamic nation under his rule. Although in the past Jews have done well under Arab rule, the belief in a united Arab nation leaves no room for the existence of a Jewish state right in the middle of what they believe is their territory. However, as Isaiah 19:23-25 indicates, the Middle East cannot be a blessing without the rebirth of Israel (which happened in 1948) and the eventual reconciliation of Jews and Arabs. In the 1930s Arab Christian prophets in Jordan were prophesying Israel would be reborn, but were quieted by western replacement theology missionaries who did not agree.

It is interesting to note that the Middle East includes nine strategic cities situated in the shape of a cross. Colossians 2:15 tells us that all the principalities and powers of this world are overcome by the cross. Jesus died in Jerusalem, in the heart of the Middle East, and this is where Isaiah 19 will be fulfilled. Islam and Judaism will be shaken to their very foundations, and they will recognize Jesus as their Messiah. Of the nine strategic cities, Ankara (Turkey), Beirut (Lebanon), Damascus (Syria), Amman (Jordan), Medina and Mecca (Saudi Arabia) form the vertical bar of the cross. The cities forming the horizontal bar of the cross are Cairo (Egypt), Jerusalem (Israel) and Baghdad (Iraq). (See map 4, page 190.)

It is clear that the Gospel of Jesus Christ will triumph over the anti-Messiah aspects in Islam and Judaism. As we pray and boldly proclaim the Gospel, the Arab as well as Jewish peoples will be delivered from the curses put upon them. Together they will become a blessing in the midst of the earth.

Because the peace of Jerusalem represents the ultimate reconciliation and restoration of the world according to God's order and purposes, this issue is rooted very deep in the hearts and minds of Jews, Arabs and other people not only throughout history but also those living today. Within God's peace process, the Prince of Peace, through His redemptive sacrifice, will bridge the deepest rifts between individuals and people groups. Such a division is the one that separates the Muslims and the Jews today.

As we intercede for the peace of Jerusalem, we need to realize that our battle is not against religious Jews who control much of Jerusalem. Nor is our battle against Muslims who control the Temple Mount. Our battle is not against flesh and blood, no matter how real, strong and negative these groups are about faith in the Messiah Yeshua. Our battle is against the anti-Messiah spirit that is blinding both Jew and Arab. This is the ultimate battle.

One of the essential components preparing the way for His kingdom is Jewish–Arab reconciliation in Messiah. God wants to remove the anti-

Christ spirit of Islam and the blindness to the Messiah that is oppressing the Jewish people in Jerusalem and throughout Israel.

> **"And I will pour out on the house of David and the inhabitants of Jerusalem a spirit of grace and supplication. They will look on me, the one they have pierced, and they will mourn for him as one mourns for an only child, and grieve bitterly for him as one grieves for a firstborn son" (Zechariah 12:10).**

Here God promises that He will pour out His Spirit upon the house of David and the inhabitants of Jerusalem. Since 1967, thousands of Jewish people in Israel and the nations have received the Lord. But why does He add, "and the inhabitants of Jerusalem?" This is because there will be many Arab and international believers in Jerusalem as well. God is going to open up the fountain upon the house of David (the Jewish people) and also upon the Arabs and all the inhabitants of Jerusalem.

Egypt and Israel

As we saw in chapter 5, there is reason to believe that the Garden of Eden spread from Egypt (the Pishon River), Ethiopia and Sudan (the Gihon River) in the south, all the way to the Tigris and Euphrates Rivers in what is now modern-day Iran and Iraq. We also know that the first two major civilizations on earth were centered in the areas of Egypt and Assyria. The major events in the history of God's purposes for His people took place in this entire region, from the Nile to the Euphrates.

The first two rivers mentioned in the Garden of Eden appear to be in the region of Egypt. Abraham went down to Egypt, as did Jacob and all of his sons, because of the great famine that plagued their land. Joseph became a respected man in Egypt, second in authority and power only to Pharaoh himself. The children of Israel were in Egypt for 400 years. Abraham met Hagar there, and this Egyptian woman became the mother of Ishmael. Moses brought the children of Israel out of Egypt. God chose to give them His law from Mount Sinai, which is a part of Egypt. The link between Egypt and Israel is ancient; there has always been a highway that has connecting these two lands.

In what marked the beginnings of a major move of God in our ministry, we sent a prayer team down to the Sinai in 1985. (See chapter 6 for detailed results of this trip.) Egypt is very significant in God's purposes.

The presence of the Lord was in the Garden of Eden. When Adam was cast out, he might not have been cast out of a physical place at all but rather cast out of the presence of God. In the original Garden of Eden, I believe it was as if the heavens and the earth were as one. Adam had an open heaven above him, but when he was cast out of the presence of God, the heavens closed up on him.

There is a possibility that when Abraham walked from Assyria to Israel to Egypt, and then back again to Israel, he was not building any new highway between these places but he was rebuilding ancient altars. It might very well be that he was merely re-laying foundations for something that had existed from the very beginning—the Garden of Eden. Whether Abraham was building or rebuilding what had been founded in the Garden of Eden, we know that God is presently building and will ultimately establish a strong link between Egypt, Israel and Assyria. We can tell Abraham had a vision of the connection between these three places because of the way he walked through the land.

The prophet Isaiah writes:

> "Listen to me, you who pursue righteousness and who seek the Lord: Look to the rock from which you were cut and to the quarry from which you were hewn; look to Abraham, your father, and to Sarah, who gave you birth. When I called him he was but one, and I blessed him and made him many. The Lord will surely comfort Zion and will look with compassion on all her ruins; he will make her deserts like Eden, her wastelands like the garden of the Lord. Joy and gladness will be found in her, thanksgiving and the sound of singing" (Isaiah 51:1-3).

Here, the prophet says, "Look to Abraham, your father, and Sarah, who gave you birth. When I called him, he was alone but I blessed him and made him many." We know that Sarah gave birth to Isaac, who produced many sons, including Jacob, whose name was later changed to Israel. "I blessed him and made him many." Abraham also had children through Ishmael. The prophet goes on to say something very interesting. He speaks of comforting Zion. This scripture appears to refer mainly to Israel. However, God does not say "desert" or "wasteland" in the singular. He is speaking of many places, not merely the Negev desert as we know it now. We could imagine that He was seeing beyond Israel in this context. Nevertheless, He will make deserts like Eden and the wastelands like the gardens of the Lord. This directly has to do with the restoration of all things. Israel and the Middle East will be restored "like the Garden of Eden" when the holy city, the new Jerusalem comes down from heaven.

Assyria and Israel

Assyria was a place of great biblical and historical significance. We know that Noah's ark landed on Mount Ararat, in modern-day Turkey, a part of the former Assyrian Empire. Abraham came out of Assyria, from Haran which is just a few kilometers from Mount Ararat. It is interesting to note that the patriarchs lived their whole life on this highway from Assyria to Egypt. Abraham went down to Egypt and returned to live in Hebron, a center of violent dispute between Arab and Jew to this day.

In every major town along this highway, there is a major Jewish community as a well as an Arab community. The people live separately, Arabs in one location and Jews in another. There are Arabic and Jewish quarters in Beth El and Ramallah, in Shechem and Nablus, and in Kiryat Arba and Hebron. The common phrases "East Jerusalem" and "West Jerusalem" are reminders of the separation between Muslims and Jews. Each group is saying that it has exclusive rights to some or all of the ancient cities and sites. Much of the terrorist activity and *intifada* attacks take place along this highway. The Jews are saying their way is best, and the Muslims are saying that their way is best.

If we look even deeper at the history of this highway, we learn more about the relationship that existed among the different nations. When the Patriarchs wanted to marry, they went up to Assyria in the North, selected their wives, and brought them back down. There was constant movement along the highway. The exodus out of Egypt moved along this highway, and Israel was born. The exodus to Babylon and the return back to Israel also moved along this highway. The climax of the last exodus from Russia is coming from Assyria to Israel, the other direction on the highway. The first Christian church was established in Antioch, which was in the region of Assyria. We can say that the most significant numbers of Jews to return to Israel, past and future, are coming from Egypt and Assyria into Jerusalem and Israel. This highway is going to be the highway of reconciliation, the highway of salvation:

> **"There will be a highway for the remnant of his people that is left from Assyria, as there was for Israel when they came up from Egypt" (Isaiah 11:15).**

The wise men who visited the child Jesus after His birth came from Assyria. Some scholars believe that the Magi, who came following the star, looking for Jesus to be born, were the Medes, modern-day Kurds. Many Kurds live in northern Iraq. Saddam Hussein declared war against them during the 1990s and sought to destroy them. In the face of such horror, many are turning away from Islam and towards the Lord. They are hanging pictures of Jesus in their homes. Some are not yet believers, but are doing this as an act of rebellion. The Magi who went looking for Jesus are now finding Him, as God is pouring out His Spirit and drawing the Kurds to Himself. In Matthew 2:1, we see the Magi coming from the East. In verse 13, Jesus escapes down into Egypt, going the other direction on the highway to fulfill what the prophet said: **"Out of Egypt I called my son" (Matthew 2: 15; Hosea 11:1).**

Jordan, which was part of biblical Assyria, is also a place of significance because it was the inheritance of two-and-a-half tribes of Israel after the Israelites came out of Egypt. We also know this is where Ruth, who joined with Naomi, was from. Many of the Jewish believers and Jewish people who escaped from Jerusalem when it was destroyed in 70 AD settled in Pella, Jordan, and it appears that in these last days Jordan again may be a place of protection for God's people (Dan. 11:41–12:13; Rev. 11: 2, 12:12) and that the Jews and Arabs will be sheltered together in Jordan (Isa. 16:1-5).

God has begun to restore the age-old foundations of His peace process, which includes the return of the Jewish people from both directions on the highway, from Egypt and Assyria, to join those from the four corners of the earth with the King on His throne in Jerusalem. The process also includes the reconciliation of Jews and Arabs in Israel in the name of the Living God. It includes the Arabs and Jews who live on both sides of the highway. They will worship God together. This is slowly becoming a spiritual reality reflective of God's ultimate redemptive purposes for this region. God's original intention is reflected in the Garden of Eden before the Fall. The only way that peace will come to the Middle East in the midst of so much turmoil is through a revelation of the Prince of Peace. Peace will not come if we compromise the Word of God and accept the plans of man. Peace will not come to the Middle East if we deny that *aliyah* is part of this process (see Stones 3 and 4). God's peace plan will not be fulfilled if the Jews deny the reality of God in order to pursue political solutions. It will only be pursued as we realize that one of the strategic end-time purposes of God is to unite Jews, Arabs and Gentiles together in the person of Messiah.

If we want to be involved in the purposes of God, we cannot compromise. We need to stand, not only with the Prince of Peace and His reconciling purposes, but with *aliyah* and with the boundaries that God has set forth in His Word. His Word will not return void, but accomplish the purposes for which it was intended.

Ultimately, God will have His way. Many things are being shaken today, and judgment is occurring because of compromise. We know that God is watching over Israel. He is looking for the coming of His Kingdom in the Middle East and on earth as it is in heaven. With our natural mind, it is almost impossible to imagine that those traditional barriers of hate and division can be broken down. However, even the age-old boundaries will be broken down in the Kingdom of God. We already have a part of the Kingdom of God with us because the Holy Spirit is with us. This is a down payment of our inheritance.

This message of the unity of the Kingdom of God runs throughout the Old and New Covenants, and has always been central to the heart of

God. The Jews proclaim the unity of God each time they recite the *Sh'ma*: "**Hear O Israel, the** L<small>ORD</small> **is God, the** L<small>ORD</small> **is one**" **(Deuteronomy 6:4)**. Arabs are also for this kind of unity and they too proclaim that there is one God. But only in the oneness of the true God and through the blood of the sacrificed Lamb can all the differences of mankind be reconciled and resolved.

Isaiah 9 outlines the beginning of the peace process and tells us that the Child that is born is the Son that is given, the "**Wonderful Counselor, the Mighty God, the Everlasting Father, the Prince of Peace.**" Jesus taught us to pray, saying, "Our Father, which art in heaven … Thy Kingdom come, Thy will be done, on earth as it is in heaven." The answer to this prayer is prophesied by Zechariah:

> "**The** L<small>ORD</small> **will be king over the whole earth. On that day there will be one Lord and his name the only name**" (Zechariah 14:9).

Jesus proclaimed the Kingdom of God over 100 times during His ministry. When He returns to reign as King in Jerusalem, this prayer will be fulfilled. Everything will be shaken that can be shaken and whatever that is in us that is part of the Kingdom of God will remain. Not only will people be shaken personally, the Church and Israel will be shaken to their foundations. We need the cross to deal with everything in our lives that is not under the rule of the Kingdom of God. The Kingdom of God, which cannot be shaken, will last forever.

May the Prince of Peace and the King of Jerusalem, Messiah Jesus, come soon to Jerusalem to take up the Throne of David, to the Temple Mount, the place of the soles of His feet forever. Pray that He will restore all things, including the fullness of the Tabernacle of David, the one new man, Arab and Jew, and the remnant of all nations.

Stone 3:
Return of the Jewish People to Israel

The return of the Jews to Israel is central to the heart of God. God promised that Abraham's descendants would inherit the land that He had given. This promise is meant to be taken literally. Over 700 Bible verses speak of the return of the Jews to Israel. This is explained in my first book, *Let My People Go!* An integral part of God's purposes and for the ultimate peace of Jerusalem is the return of His people to the Middle East. Yet from a humanist perspective this is difficult to imagine in the natural and in the light of challenges in the land. Humanists may also argue that the return of the Jews is counterproductive to peace, since an influx of Jews to Israel can raise a problem for Muslims. Yet the physical land of Israel and the flesh-and-blood Jewish people remain important to God's purposes.

Sadly, and despite the fact that the return of the Jews is biblical, this event does cause great distress to some Arabs. In reality, the more Jews return, the more we should rejoice because their return is an indication of the fulfillment of God's plan for reconciliation. There is also more than adequate land in Israel for all the Jews in the world and all the Arab Palestinians who want to live here. There are six million people living in Hong Kong. Israel is 20 times bigger than Hong Kong. Justice for Arab Palestinians and *aliyah* are not contradictory but should be complementary to God's purposes of reconciliation and restoration. We need to see *aliyah* through God's eyes, because His ways are higher than our ways.

History has already proven the disastrous effects of these humanistic concerns. When the land of Israel was still under the British Mandate and not yet an independent country, Arabs protested the arrival of so many Jews from Eastern Europe. As the Jewish population increased, they knew that their control over the land would be directly challenged. The Arab nations united in influencing Britain into limiting immigration into Palestine. Britain bowed to the pressure and justified her decision on political and economic grounds. Most of those wanting to enter Palestine at that time were refugees from the concentration camps of Eastern Europe. Britain's solution was to take Jews from the ghettos and concentration camps of Europe and put them in a different set of camps on the island of Cyprus, also behind barbed wires, to wait.

The Jews refused to accept this situation and, until Israel officially became an independent state, they smuggled their own people into the land at night and under the cover of darkness. Today, some Arabs continue to maintain that increased immigration poses a threat to the political peace process, although God's plan for the return of the Jews to Israel is one of reconciliation. In these end times, God is bringing the Jewish people back to Israel from the four corners of the earth:

> "In that day the Lord will reach out his hand a second time to reclaim the remnant that is left of his people from Assyria, from Lower Egypt, from Upper Egypt, from Cush, from Elam, from Babylon, from Hamath and from the islands of the sea [the Americas].
>
> He will raise a banner for the nations and gather the exiles of Israel; he will assemble the scattered people of Judah from the four quarters of the earth.
>
> Ephraim's jealousy will vanish, and Judah's enemies will be cut off; Ephraim will not be jealous of Judah, nor Judah hostile toward Ephraim. They will swoop down on the slopes of Philistia to the west; together they will plunder the people to the east. They will lay hands on Edom and Moab, and the Ammonites will be subject to them. The Lord will dry up the gulf of the Egyptian Sea; with a scorching wind he will sweep his hand over the Euphrates River. He will break it up into seven streams so that men can cross over in sandals.
>
> There will be a highway for the remnant of his people that is left from Assyria, as there was for Israel when they came up from Egypt" (Isaiah 11:11-16).

> "However, the days are coming," declares the Lord, "when men will no longer say, 'As surely as the Lord lives, who brought the Israelites up out of Egypt,' but they will say, 'As surely as the Lord lives, who brought the Israelites up out of the land of the north and out of all the countries where he had banished them.'

**For I will restore them to the land I gave to their forefathers"
(Jeremiah 16:14-15).**

During *Pesach* (Passover), the Jewish people traditionally remember the exodus from Egypt. In Jeremiah 16, we read that another exodus from the lands of the North will be far greater than the exodus that Moses led. It is even written that the Jewish people will change the way they refer to God, no longer calling Him the God who led His people out of Egypt. He will be known as the God who delivered His people from the North and all the lands to which He had scattered them. It is hard to imagine something more incredible than God's parting of the Red Sea to let three million Jews pass through and then closing the waters again.

In Ezekiel, the Lord spoke of how He is going to gather His people from all the nations back to Israel. He said He would join them together in the land—bone to bone, flesh to flesh. He will put flesh on them and will breathe on them by the Holy Ghost. They will be raised up as an exceedingly great army. A small number of Jewish people are now turning to the Lord in the nations of the world, and more will come to Him in the future. But most will return as dry bones, as people who are spiritually dead, not born again by the spirit of God. Ninety-eight percent of the Jews returning from Russia come back with no or little faith in God and very little, if any, understanding of their Jewish roots. When the Lord says that they will not see Him again until they say, "Blessed is he, who comes in the name of the Lord," He refers to a spiritual rebirth of large proportions. He is talking of Jews coming to know their Messiah.

It is clear that these prophecies will be fulfilled in a special way, in that the last exodus will manifest in ways not seen in the first. First, the Jews who have returned to Israel will receive their Messiah. Second, when they do, the clouds of heaven will not be able to hold the Messiah back! The Father will release Him from heaven; He will put His feet on the Mount of Olives and take up His throne in Jerusalem.

Shaking All That Can Be Shaken

The book of Isaiah contains the most prophecies in the Bible about the

Prince of Peace and God's end-time purposes. In Isaiah 2, the prophet speaks of Jerusalem being established as the chief of the mountains, all nations streaming into it. In Isaiah 9, we are introduced to the Prince of Peace. Then, in chapter 11, we see the Jewish people coming home from the four corners of the earth. From chapters 9 to 19, we read about the wars, judgments and shakings that will take place in the Middle East. The emphatic focus of chapter 14 on the shakings going on in the Arab countries also describes the Jews returning to their land:

> "The LORD will have compassion on Jacob; once again he will choose Israel and will settle them in their own land. ... Nations will take them and bring them to their own place"
> (Isaiah 14:1-2).

Most of the shakings prophesied between chapters 11 and 19 have not yet taken place, but the Gulf War was a first-fruit of what we can expect to happen in the future. We can expect to see things happening! These shakings will begin with the return of the Jewish people to Israel. Isaiah 11: 10-11 lists all the Arab nations from which the Jews will return. By the late 1990s most of the Jews from other Middle Eastern countries have returned to Israel. Some of those who have not returned, like those in Iran, are suffering great persecution for their faith.

God has promised that He will shake all that can be shaken. As harsh as this may be, there are three very important reasons for God's decisions. The first shaking is for the preparation of the bride of Messiah. What needs shaking from your life? What sin, bad habit or deeply ingrained attitude are you still holding on to? God will shake us until all that is ungodly within us is forced out, and only His kingdom remains within us.

The second reason for the shaking is the salvation of unbelievers. Through difficulties and hard times, He is shaking them right into the Kingdom of God. When people are comfortable, they usually won't admit their need for help. It is easier to turn to God in the midst of extremely harsh circumstances. It is His plan that people become desperate for God. It is the mercy of God that shakes the things of the world right out of us and brings us into His Kingdom!

As related to this chapter, the third and primary reason for shakings is to convince the Jewish people to leave the countries where they have lived so comfortably for so long, and bring them back to Israel. Over 700 Bible verses cannot be wrong. God will bring His people back. Through His prophet Amos, God declared,

> **"I will bring back my exiled people Israel; they will rebuild the ruined cities and live in them. They will plant vineyards and drink their wine; they will make gardens and eat their fruit. I will plant Israel in their own land, never again to be uprooted from the land I have given them" (Amos 9:14-15).**

We are living in the time of the last exodus to Israel. The Jews will never be uprooted again. Only those moving to countries other than Israel will be uprooted and maybe some will be in refuge in Jordan during the time of the anti-Christ, but even Jordan is part of the Promised Land (Dan. 11:41). For those moving directly to Israel, it is the last return.

Gathering from the North, West, South and East

In 1986, I led a prayer team of 'fishers' to Moscow and the first thing the Lord directed us to do was a Jericho March around the Kremlin. I was afraid, thinking that if I did this I would end up in Siberia. It turned out to be not so difficult after all. Since the Communists did not believe in God, they did not care if a group of foreigners prayed at their governmental headquarters—as long as we did not involve the Russian citizens in prayer as well. Our group of intercessors did a Jericho March around the Kremlin, all the while praying in the spirit for the walls of Communism to come down and for the Gospel of Jesus Christ to penetrate Russia. Many people worldwide were praying with us at that time.

Only 200 Jewish people had come out of Russia in 1986, but about one week after our Jericho March that year, the Communists agreed to release 12,000 people. Praise God that these came out over the next year.

In 1996, ten years later, I led another Jericho March around the Kremlin just before critical elections in which the old line Communists were opposing President Yeltsin and the supporters of Democracy. Pastors and believers from Moscow joined us in prayer, and the Communists were stopped.

God has subsequently released approximately one million Jews to Israel from the land of the North as we have done ten Jericho Marches around the Kremlin over 15 years from 1986 to 2000. The tenth one we did was during Passover in April 2000. We did it believing God to bring about the fullness of the return of His people home from the lands of the North and to open up the first-fruit from the West.

One day as I was praying, the Lord showed me trains and planes going back to Israel. The locomotive was coming out of Russia, and was on its way to Israel. This train was not going to Auschwitz; it was going to freedom and true liberation in Israel. During an earlier visit to Auschwitz, I remember reading a sign that said, "He who does not learn the lessons of history is doomed to repeat them." Unfortunately, about 90 percent of the Jewish people were killed in the Holocaust because they did not heed the warning to leave while they yet could.

On the trains and planes in the vision, there were people from many countries in the world. God is gathering His people home.

I believe God wants to raise up rabbis as true shepherds who will call and lead their people back to their land and their God. In Cologne, Germany, in 1891, when Hitler was a young boy, Dr. Badenhelmer heard a voice from heaven ringing in his ear, saying, "Save my people, lest they die." It was a true prophetic warning to the Jews. But during the 1930s and 1940s, while most of the prophetic voices of the Jewish and Christian watchmen were crying out in Europe, most rabbis not only remained, but also discouraged Jews from leaving. They were afraid to upset the status quo although the warning cries had started long before then, even at the end of the 19th century. The individuals urging rapid departure included Jabotinsky, who cried out that the Jews should leave because the fire was burning under their feet. Max Nordin told His people, "Liquidate the Diaspora among the nations, or the nations will liquidate you."

In the mid-1990s, the Chief Rabbi of Syria made *aliyah* to Israel. I recently met with him. When he went to Damascus from New York, they thought he was going to stay. He said: "No, I am on my way home to Israel and then I will call all the Syrian Jews worldwide to return to the land of Israel." Today, very few Jews remain in Syria. As we see anti-Semitism arising in different parts of the world today, we need to pray that God will touch the rabbis, and that they will lead His people home as this rabbi from Syria did. We need to pray that they will not be false shepherds leading their people to destruction as happened during the Holocaust in Europe but that they act instead as true shepherds leading their people back to their land and their God.

The exodus that God is talking about in Jeremiah is not limited to Russia and the North, for besides **"the land of the north"** the Lord adds, **"and all the countries where He had banished them" (Jeremiah 16:15).** Moreover, as with the Jews who returned from Egypt, none will be left behind (Ezek. 39:27-28). When all the Jews return from the United States, France and Great Britain, it will be a bigger miracle than the Jews coming out of Egypt. As surely as the Lord has shaken the nations of the former Soviet Union, He will shake the nations of the West. God is bringing His people home from other nations as well, and in ways that clearly indicate His sovereignty.

As Communism was falling, I took a trip to the former Yugoslavia, which is now divided into five different countries. The Lord told us to warn the Jewish people to leave their country. We talked to the Chief Rabbi and many other individuals and encouraged them to come home. They refused to go, believing that they had a secure future since the fall of Communism. Two months later disaster struck in the form of violent persecution, and thousands fled for their lives.

We have seen equally vivid reminders of God's seriousness in bringing the Jews to Israel literally from the four corners of the world. In many countries of the world where Jews live today, there is turmoil. God is beginning to shake the nations. At one time, God's voice shook only the earth, but now He has promised, **"Once more I will shake not only the earth but also the heavens" (Hebrews 12:26; Haggai 2:6).** As surely as God has shaken the former Soviet Union, He is going to shake the West to release His people to Israel.

> "This is what the Lord says to me:
>
> 'Go, post a lookout and have him report what he sees. When he sees chariots with teams of horses, riders on donkeys, or riders on camels, let him be alert, fully alert.'
>
> 'And the lookout shouted,
>
> 'Day after day, my lord, I stand on the watchtower; every night I stay at my post. Look, here comes a man in a chariot with a team of horses. And he gives back the answer: Babylon has fallen, has fallen! All the images of its gods lie shattered on the ground!'
>
> "O my people, crushed on the threshing floor, I tell you what I have heard from the LORD Almighty, from the God of Israel" (Isaiah 21:6-10).

In Hosea 11:10-11, the Lord says,

> "'They shall walk after the LORD. He will roar like a lion. When he roars, then his sons shall come trembling from the west, they shall come trembling like a bird from Egypt, like a dove from the land of Assyria. And I will let them dwell in their houses,' says the LORD."

This passage in Isaiah challenges us to be watchmen constantly on the alert. It talks about watching because Babylon is falling. I believe we live in the days when Babylon in the West is going to fall. God is going to bring economic hardships to the United States, France and Great Britain. It has already begun to happen in certain parts of the world. When the Asian markets collapsed, the world went into a state of panic. As the gods of materialism, wealth and prosperity collapse, people will be released to put their trust in God. The strongholds that are holding the Jews back in the West must be broken. They must be released to turn their eyes to Messiah and Jerusalem, sparking a massive *aliyah* from the West, which could be an exodus even greater than the exodus out of Egypt.

Early in 1987, while praying in our house of prayer in Washington, D.C., I received a vision of judgments coming on America. Bombs were exploding, and I saw Islamic terrorists coming against America. There possibly were Communists along with them. Islamic terrorists are causing bombs to explode in different parts of the world today, including the United States. The Lord told me that it was time for the American Jewish people to return to Israel. He said to warn them and encourage them to come home.

The United States has been good to the over six million Jews who live there. However, God did not say, "I chose Miami, or Los Angeles, or New York." He did not even choose Paris. Many Jews probably wish God had chosen New York. It would have been a lot easier because almost as many Jewish people live in New York as in Israel.

I initially thought that the Jews were spiritually and physically bound in Russia, but that they were free to leave the United States. In 1987, on one of my trips to the former Soviet Union, I asked the Lord why the Jews hadn't returned to Israel from America in greater numbers. The Lord revealed to me that the Jews in America were in even greater bondage than the Russian Jews. I found this hard to believe at first until the Lord directed me to Ephesians 6:12:

> **"For our struggle is not against flesh and blood, but against the rulers, against the authorities, against the powers of this dark world and against the spiritual forces of evil in the heavenly realms."**

This has proven to be quite true regarding the Jews. Almost one million Jews have returned to Israel from the former Soviet Union since the end of 1989. Only a handful of Jews have returned from America.

One reason He has shaken South Africa so strongly is to bring the Jews home. Several years ago, there was a severe famine in Ethiopia and the Jews began returning to Israel. They are also coming back from Morocco, Syria and India. Even the few Jews left in China will return.

God will remain faithful to His word. In the last few years, I have met many Americans who have only recently learned that they are Jewish. Because of the Holocaust, their parents hid their tragic past from their children. Nevertheless, God is revealing hidden identities because He will bring His people back to the land of Israel.

I believe that as surely as the Lord is uncovering the Jews in the West, He will begin to uncover the lost tribes in the East, even those deeply hidden in Islam. Some people believe that the ten lost tribes are hidden within Muslim countries, in Pakistan, India and Afghanistan. I talked to people in India who have met Muslims who light candles every Friday night and have placed a *mezuzah* (the Bible scripture containing the *Sh'ma* housed in a small cylinder) on their door posts. While in India, we prayed for the Benei–Israel Jews in Bombay to come home to Israel, and also that God would bring visions and dreams of the highway leading back to Jerusalem to the people of the ten lost tribes.

Fishers and Hunters

> "'I will restore them to the land I gave their forefathers. But now I will send for many fishermen', declares the LORD, 'and they will catch them. After that, I will send for many hunters, and they will hunt them down on every mountain and hill and from the crevices of the rocks'" (Jeremiah 16:15-16).

God has called all believers to be fishermen. Jesus said to His disciples, "I will make you fishers of men if you follow me." Hundreds of thousands from among His own people and millions from the nations have heeded this call, and the Gospel has spread around the globe.

The prophet Jeremiah spoke specifically about the return of the Jews to Israel in the last days (Jer. 16:14-16). In this passage, he highlights the need for fishers. In the hands of Jesus, ordinary people can become fishers. Once these fishers have done their duty to bring in the harvest, Jeremiah says there will be hunters who hunt down those not willing to respond to the call of the fishers. Such was the lot of the Jews who did not heed the call to leave Poland 60 years ago.

Discerning the Hunters

Islamic Fundamentalism is one form of shaking that God is allowing in these times. A report of an Islamic Fundamentalist meeting held in Paris told of a "new assertiveness" demonstrated by Muslims across Europe. Among their demands are Koranic schools for their children and the loosening of immigration restrictions. France, which has the largest Muslim population in Europe (over five million), has not been receptive to Muslims' demands. Even Islamic organizations in France fear manipulation by extremists outside of the country, believing that they could become a time bomb that will explode in a single day, according to newspaper reports.

Islamic Fundamentalism has also grown rapidly in the United States. In 1995, Louis Farrakhan and other Nation of Islam leaders organized a Million Man March on the nation's capital. Many black Christians were made to feel that they were selling out their race if they did not participate in the march. After the march, Farrakhan stated that he is going to establish the nation of Islam on American soil. He then went to visit Omar Khadaffi in Libya, Saddam Hussein in Iraq, and leaders in Iran in order to raise money for his initiatives.

Meanwhile, terrorism is escalating in America. In 1999 in Littleton, Colorado, two neo-Nazi students killed 13 other students on Hitler's birthday, which also happens to be Israel's birthday. The increase of global economic instability poses a serious problem for the Jews. Throughout history, the Jews have always been blamed for economic problems. It is time for the Jews in the West to heed the warning in Hosea 11.

Five Ways Fishers Can Help

There are five concrete steps fishers can take to help fulfill God's promise to bring His people back to their land. But all five of these steps must be taken in the spirit of Joshua and Caleb. One of the primary reasons why more Jewish people have not made *aliyah* from the West sooner than they did from other nations of the world, is because of the evil reports of many people similar to those by the ten spies. Rather than choosing to see that Israel is a good land, flowing with milk and honey, where God manifested

His son Yeshua as a sacrifice and will be manifested in all of His goodness at the second coming of His Son, many people who visited Israel identified with the ten spies. They could have seen that they were more than able to overcome the problems. Instead, they chose to see the giants. Many Jewish people listened to the evil report of the ten and do not rise up in faith to possess the land. What is needed today, are watchmen, worshipers, intercessors and fishers with the Joshua and Caleb spirit who will break the forces of unbelief off the Jewish people in the nations. This will break open the gates of their cities and encourage them to be Joshuas and Calebs to enter in and possess the land naturally and spiritually for their Messiah.

1. *Pray:* The Lord says that He will bring people to His holy mountain and give them joy in His house of prayer. He will make His house a house of prayer for all nations (Isaiah 56:7). He then declares that He will gather the exiles of Israel that have not yet been gathered (v.8). We need to pray for the Jewish people in all nations to be gathered back to Israel.

2. *Warn:* As fishers we need to warn the Jewish people. *Let My People Go!*, the book I wrote about *aliyah*, has now been translated into 24 languages. Some people believe that fishermen need bait and tens of thousands of people have given this book to their Jewish neighbors. God wants His fishermen to present His truth to the Jews in different countries, encouraging them to come back to their homeland while they can do so with their resources.

3. *Help Jews Financially to Make Aliyah:* Isaiah 49:22 says that God will beckon to the Gentiles, and that they will carry the Jews back to Israel on their shoulders. In the first century, the Jews took the Gospel to the Gentiles in the four corners of the earth. Now, it is time for the Gentiles to come to the assistance of the Jews.

4. *Help in a Time of Prevention, Not of Calamity:* In the past, Jews have mostly returned to Israel in a time of crisis, desperation and calamity. Jews who make plans to leave today can do so with their financial resources intact and with time to make the necessary plans to

establish themselves in their new home. They can come ready to take part in and eventually contribute to Israeli life. Those who wait and eventually come in a time of crisis are usually forced to flee in haste, leaving their possessions behind. We need to be delivered from the mentality that the only way the Jewish people will leave the West is in a time of calamity. We need to rise up in faith, worship and intercession to bring about a breakthrough that will bring the Jews back in a time of prevention and not just in a time of calamity.

5.   *Prepare to Help During Calamity:* For those Jews in the United States and millions of others around the world who are unwilling to come back in a time of prevention. The Church needs to prepare for the time of calamity and crisis. Underground railroads are being prepared to help His people in time of crisis. Hundreds of people are preparing places of refuge for the Jews in the United States and other countries.

In His mercy, God sends the fishers to help His people return to Israel. Who are the fishers? They are the people who are doing all they can to help the Jews return to Israel. They can warn people, they can instruct them on God's plan; and they can actually help them physically. Many reading this book are potential fishermen if not already involved in such work. God is calling people in His kingdom for such a time as this.

Psalm 102:16 says when the Lord builds up Zion, He will appear in His glory. As we pray and work for *aliyah*, we are praying for the peace of Jerusalem.

Stone 4:
Return of Jewish Believers to Israel

"The ransomed (redeemed) of the LORD shall return. They will enter Zion with singing; everlasting joy will crown their heads. Gladness and joy will overtake them, and sorrow and sighing will flee away" (Isaiah 51:11).

There have been Jewish believers living in Israel throughout the 20th century, although very few until 1967—the year that marked the reunification of Jerusalem as well as the beginning of the time when the fig tree began to blossom (Luke 21). Before 1967, there were only a handful of Messianic congregations in Israel; now the number has grown to about 80, and the number of Messianic believers has grown to between 6,000 and 10,000. Thousands of Messianic Jews have come back from Russia and hundreds from Ethiopia. Both groups are a tremendous blessing to the Body of Messiah here. Hundreds of *sabras* (native-born Israelis) have received Jesus as their Messiah.

As we have already discussed in the section on *aliyah*, over 700 scriptures speak of God bringing His people back to their homeland in the days of restoration. But, while there are hundreds of thousands of Messianic believers in the United States, why are there not more in Israel?

1.   *The Timing of God:* One reason is that worldwide renewal is moving from the ends of the earth back to Jerusalem; we believe that the Spirit will soon be poured out upon Israel in God's perfect timing. The fire of revival in the first century went from Jerusalem to the ends of the earth. Today God is moving in fire from the ends of the earth back to Jerusalem. At All Nations Convocation Jerusalem 2000 we brought torches from the nations back to Jerusalem and gave it to Jewish and Arab people in Israel. This was a prophetic act, signalling the return of the fire that went from Jerusalem to the nations 2,000 years ago.

2.   *The Comforts of the Home Nation:* The comforts and materialism of
      the West have affected Messianic believers just as they have affected
      other Jews living in America and Western Europe. Pulling up roots,
      leaving the place where they grew up, and moving to another cul-
      ture is very difficult. Learning Hebrew, adjusting to a country always
      in the midst of crisis, serving in the military or knowing that their
      children will have to serve in the armed forces, and finding a profes-
      sional niche are all overwhelming hurdles which confront anyone
      making *aliyah* to Israel. Most individuals who move to Israel from
      the West automatically accept a drop in their standard of living. One
      prevalent joke among immigrants in Israel today asks the question,
      "How do you make a small fortune in Israel?" The answer, closer to
      the truth than many would like to admit, is, "Come with a big for-
      tune." Yet, this should not be true among believers if they have been
      delivered from the love of money. They love God and are committed
      to lay down their lives for the God of Israel and His purposes.

3.   *Bound by Materialism:* For a person from the West to make *aliyah*,
      they have to have a strong sense of commitment to what the Word
      of God says about *aliyah,* and the call of God revealed in the Bible
      has to be greater than the comforts of life in the United States. Once
      they arrive here, a strong commitment to Israel is essential in order
      to help the new immigrants be overcomers.

      Some American Jews say that they are not called to Israel.
However, we know that the call of the Jews to return to the land
of their fathers is a call inherent in the Bible. Paul Lieberman, an
American Jewish believer, admits that he originally had no sense of
calling to Israel, even after he accepted the Messiah. However, he
was challenged to pray and ask God if it were not His will. As he
started praying and searching the Bible, he felt a very deep calling
to his homeland and is now part of the leadership of a Messianic
congregation in Netanya, Israel. I have spoken to many Messianic
Jews who tell me that, after reading *Let My People Go!* and praying
the scriptures on the back of the book, they saw the scriptures of
aliyah in a new light. His Word became real to them. God's Word is

like a hammer, like fire and more powerful than a two-edged sword. It can break off the materialistic bondage as well as the fears and the insecurities of starting over.

One reason that Messianic Jews have returned in such large numbers from the former Soviet Union is that life in Israel is more attractive to them than in their homelands. When asked a direct question, however, many do admit that America would have been their first choice but that it was not realistic to think of getting there. Until natural life in Israel becomes more attractive than in the West, or until spiritual life and renewal in Israel becomes so deep that people are drawn as to a flame, we will not see a massive *aliyah* from the West. Few people will want to uproot themselves and their families to start life all over again in a foreign land. Few will want to accept the challenges of a new language, of a lesser (immigrant) status and of starting over professionally. Now only those with strong Zionist tendencies or pioneer natures will brave the challenges and come. And even with great zeal, the challenges are still daunting.

4.   *Chains Not Broken by Intercessors:* Intercessors need to break the chains of materialism off the Jews in the West. God called the prophet Jeremiah to write in a book that God will **"bring [His] people Israel and Judah back from captivity and restore them to the land [He] gave their forefathers to possess" (Jeremiah 30: 1-3)**. Today, intercessors and watchmen need to do the same. We need to be empowered by the Lord to **"uproot and tear down, to destroy and overthrow, to build and to plant" (Jeremiah 1:10)**. We need to trust Jesus, the faithful Shepherd, the **"One who breaks open the way"** to go before the Jewish people, and they will **"break through the gate and go out" (Micah 2:13)**. Pray that the chains will soon be removed.

5.   *The Challenge of the Law:* Another great obstacle to the *aliyah* of Jewish believers is the way Messianic Jews are viewed in Israel. In 1967, the Israeli government passed a law that said that anyone who converts to another religion is no longer Jewish. Conveniently, this is

applied virtually only to Jews who have made a commitment to Jesus as their Messiah. The religious authorities consider a Jew who has become a Christian, a traitor to his heritage, and therefore no longer a Jew. We must pray that this stone is removed, because it is in direct contradiction to the Law of Return that states that any person with a Jewish parent or grandparent is eligible to return to Israel. Jews who choose to believe in Jesus, who Himself was born and lived as an observant Jew, can not be denied the right to make *aliyah*.

Of course, this has not stopped believers from moving to Israel. The biblical call to be "wise as serpents and gentle as doves" and many believers have been able to pass through the paperwork process without difficulty. The challenge usually comes in the personal interviews, when government representatives ask clever questions designed to reveal background information that might have been kept back. Since Jewish organizations keep regular files of Messianic publications, leaders in the Messianic community are usually known. One Messianic leader from the United States obtained his Israeli citizenship in Israel, and then returned later with his entire family. In the meantime, the authorities learned that he was a believer and tried to deny giving citizenship to his family as well as revoking his. For two years, his wife and children lived in the country without status, health benefits or the right to work, while the battle was conducted in the courts. God prevailed, and the members of the family are now all legally citizens of the State of Israel. However, this did not occur without a long fight and thousands of dollars in legal fees.

Spiritually, one of the biggest reasons that Messianic Jews do not make *aliyah* to Israel is that Satan is threatened when they do. He is threatened more by the second coming of Messiah than he was by the crucifixion, since, for the time being, he remains "prince of this world." When Jesus comes again, Satan will be banished forever. When Jewish believers and all Jewish people in Jerusalem and throughout Israel proclaim, "Blessed is he who comes in the name of the Lord," Satan will be finished. He is trying to stop Jewish believers from coming home and from faith in their Messiah.

Messianic believers in Israel need prayer for courage, persever-ance and great joy amidst persecution. Those congregations which have remained close to the Jewish roots of their faith and which are aggressive in reaching out and proclaiming the Gospel are subject to harassment, threats and even violence. One congregation in the north of Israel, whose focus is on outreach and aid to new immigrants from the former Soviet Union, was firebombed in the late 1990s. Their rented facilities were severely dam-aged. Two years later, they became the object of a new round of intense, calculated and persistent harassment. Every Saturday evening at the end of services, from 6 to 20 "anti-missionary" representatives stand outside the doors to intimidate and challenge the members, distribute literature, and issue threats of revoking citizenship. To Russians, raised under an evil gov-ernment, these threats are shocking reminders of a painful past. Recently, under cover of darkness during one of the evening services, 14 cars had their tires slashed. Leaders of this and other congregations receive threats, are followed and have occasionally experienced violence done to their per-sonal property. Most of them are married and have young children. These believers must be covered in our prayers for endurance, perseverance and strength as they stand strong and grow in the midst of adversity.

I liken the return of the Jewish believers to Israel to the return of the Ark of the Covenant to Jerusalem. The ark represents God's presence. It is the Jewish people who have received Jesus as their Messiah and who have been filled with the Holy Spirit who bring His presence here to Israel. It is time for the ark to come back to Jerusalem.

The battle for Jerusalem can be seen more clearly in this area than in any other. We need to pray fervently for the God of the breakthrough to break through, to remove the stones that seek to keep His people from coming home.

The reason given by most Messianic Jews in the West for not return-ing to Israel is that they want to stay in the West to share the Gospel with Jews there. I have considered this reason and partially understand their burden. The reality is that there are almost as many Jews today in Israel as there are in the United States, and yet there are 20 times more Jewish believers there than in Israel aside from the call and mandate for *aliyah*.

If God were going to equal out the laborers for the harvest, this would mean that at least 70,000 Messianic Jews from the West need to return to Israel.

It is a great blessing for Jews who know the Messiah to return to Israel. We need to pray Isaiah 51:11 as a proclamation for the release of Messianic Jews from all the nations to come to Israel. Let us pray that the Lord will hasten the day of *aliyah* of Jewish believers from the North, West and all nations so that together with those in Israel they may soon proclaim with the nation of Israel, "Blessed is he who comes in the name of the Lord." Then the redeemed of the Lord shall return and come with singing unto Zion and everlasting joy shall be upon their heads.

The salvation of Israel will bring Messiah and peace to Jerusalem. Continue to pray fervently for her salvation and her peace.

Stone 5:
Replacement Theology in the Church

Replacement Theology is a doctrine in which the importance of the physical land of Israel as well as the living, breathing Jewish people has been completely replaced by the Church.

Replacement Theology, as it has developed over the centuries, is a consequence of the Gentile Church breaking away from its biblical Jewish roots after the destruction of the Second Temple, the burning of Jerusalem and the dispersion of the Jews in 70 AD. Within one century of Jesus' death, the historical Christian Church was well on its way to separating itself from the apostolic biblical Jewish foundation in Jerusalem, although Jesus Himself was a Jew and the first believers were clearly Jews. This separation became more pronounced over the centuries.

By the third century after Jesus' death, any Jewish believer in Jesus was forced to give up his Jewish identity, forsake the observance of Jewish traditions, and renounce the links to his historic faith. For almost 2,000 years, Israel did not exist and the Church assumed the position of being God's spokesman in the world. It was the conclusion of some that God was finished with Israel since most tangible signs of its existence had disappeared.

The Bible tells us a different story. We read that God's covenant is for a thousand generations. God is a covenant-keeping God, and in 1948, He fulfilled His promise to make Israel once again a nation.

The Catholic Church nurtured the teaching of Replacement Theology. Even Martin Luther—who broke away from the Catholic Church in the 16th century because the teachings of the Church had replaced in importance the direct revelation of the Word of God—grew to have little tolerance for the Jews. Although initially eager to bring them to salvation, he became upset with them because they did not get saved fast enough. "Their tongues should be ripped out of their mouths, their passports taken away, and they should be deported from Germany," he said in response to their refusal to accept the Gospel. Although a blessing to the Gentiles, Martin Luther was a curse to the Jews, and his attitudes fostered anti-

Semitism for centuries to come. Adolph Hitler justified many of his policies on the basis of Martin Luther's earlier pronouncements and, based on the "Christ-killer" mentality that the Catholic Church held towards the Jews for years, Christians felt justified in killing Jews.

Replacement Theology tends to be more prevalent in the West, where people are more educated and where the cults of reason and science have dominated since the 15th century. Even the study of the Word of God is pursued along strict academic guidelines. Learning and knowledge are necessary, but when they become an idol in themselves and when the cult of reason becomes more important than the knowledge of the truth, people lose their passion for God's Word. In Third World countries, men and women do not have as much of a problem with this doctrine because they take the statements of the Bible literally. They do not over spiritualize biblical scriptures. When they read that God gave His promises to Abraham and his descendants, they believe that the inheritance means an actual, physical country and that the descendants of Abraham are Jewish and Arab people, the sons of Isaac and Ishmael who are alive today.

Tragically, many in the Church today live under severe deception and have stopped believing in the importance of the nation of Israel and of the Jewish people. The danger of such a theology is that, if the Church feels separate from its Jewish roots, then it is free to turn against the Jewish people and Israel. This belief system is the basis for widespread and even increasing anti-Semitism within the Church.

As we examine the doctrine of Replacement Theology, we should keep an important scriptural principle in mind. The apostle Paul talks about the natural preceding the spiritual:

> **"If there is a natural body, there is also a spiritual body... The spiritual did not come first, but the natural, and after that, the spiritual" (I Corinthians 15:44-46).**

This principle of the natural preceding the spiritual is important for us to keep in mind as we remember Israel, for in understanding this principle, we can better appreciate why God established a physical place called Israel, and a people called the Jews. It is necessary for us to take the Word of God literally and to know that God begins with the natural to end with the spiritual. From the beginning of creation, God has worked this way. Adam, the first man, was a living, breathing, natural man. Jesus, the redeemer of all mankind, was a spiritual man. We are born first as natural, living, flesh-and-blood creatures, then we are reborn of the spirit into the Kingdom of God. God came in the flesh, and took the form of a natural man, because the natural was the starting place within the creation.

Ezekiel 37 is a primary example of a scripture that begins with a natural situation and concludes with a spiritual reality. Unfortunately, many churches have not taught this passage based on the principle of the natural preceding the spiritual. The literal context of Ezekiel 37 is Israel. The coming together of dry bones indicates the revival and rebirth of the nation of Israel, and the return of the Jews from the four corners of the earth. God is now pouring out His Spirit on the Jewish people, making them alive spiritually.

This scripture can also apply to the spiritual Church, as many churches are valleys of dry bones that God is beginning to blow upon, bringing them back to life.

Dr. Larry Lea, an international prayer leader, used this chapter to pray for unbelievers to come into the Kingdom and the Church from the north, south, east and west of the world. This is the spiritual application of the scripture. But the natural application is to Israel and the Jewish people. God is working in both a natural and a spiritual way.

Another scripture related to the Jewish people, and which concerns us here, is where God declares that He will gather His children from around the world:

> **"I will say to the North, 'Give them up!' And to the South, 'Do not hold back!' Bring my sons from afar, and my daughters from the ends of the earth" (Isaiah 43:6).**

God is talking about a real return of the Jewish people from the East and West to the land of their fathers. One has only to spend a short time in

Israel today, to hear the many languages spoken in the streets, to see the different colors and cultures represented in the market places and shops, to recognize that this is happening right before our eyes.

As the Jews return to Israel in fulfillment of the promises of God, it is essential that intercessors understand the natural reality of Israel so that they can break open the way for them through prayer. For those who believe in the reality of a return of the Jews to the land of their fathers, there is an important scripture to claim. In Micah 2:12-14, God says,

> "I will surely gather all of you, O Jacob; I will surely bring together the remnant of Israel. I will bring them together like sheep in a pen, like a flock in its pasture; the place will throng with people. One who breaks open the way will go up before them; they will break through the gate, and go out. Their King will pass through before them, the LORD at their head."

Jesus is the great intercessor and we are His body. We need to watch Him and do what we see Him doing. Then we will follow Him in intercession as He breaks open the way for Israel to escape from the strongholds that keep them captive. He is the God of the breakthrough, our advocate and our chief intercessor. He said wherever we put our feet, we can possess the land for His kingdom.

This scripture is a clear illustration of the role of intercessors in breaking open the way for the Jews to return to Israel, even as Jesus broke open the way of communion with the Father. They are referred to as the people who precede the remnant of Israel and break open the way. If the way needs to be broken open, it is because it is full of obstacles, difficult to get through or even shut. Many Christian leaders around the world who have had a direct revelation of Jesus as the Messiah remain blind to the reality of the natural restoration of Israel and God's covenant purposes of working through His Church as an element in this restoration.

I believed in Replacement Theology for a number of years. As many Christians in the Western world in particular, I was blinded to the purposes of God for Israel. While I was not anti-Semitic, and was genuinely seeking the truth, I was sincerely asking the question, "Who was Israel?" From my study of the Scriptures, I had concluded that the Church had replaced Israel and had convinced others to follow this teaching as well.

In 1982, I came to Israel and spent a few weeks reading the prophets, praying, fasting and seeking God. The Lord began to lift the veil from my eyes and revealed to me His purposes for Israel. As I began to see so many promises fulfilled and so many tangible signs of God's handiwork, including divine and angelic intervention, I began to realize that God's purposes for restoration included both Israel and the Church. I began to understand the biblical perspective of hermeneutics in I Corinthians 15; that the natural comes first, to be followed by the spiritual. This principle helped me to understand that the scriptures dealing with Israel have to be taken literally, but that there can also be a spiritual application for the Church.

The time I spent in Jerusalem in 1982 was the most important time in my life other than my salvation experience. God not only gave me a revelation of His plan for Israel and the nations for the last days, He also called me to Israel to spend the future living and ministering in Jerusalem. From that time on, Jerusalem, Israel and the Jewish and Arab people have been the primary focus of my calling. Five years later, in 1987, the Lord directed me to live on the Mount of Olives in the City of the Great King.

Understanding Zion— Natural and Spiritual

The story of creation in the Bible presents a natural harmony between heaven and earth. In the Garden of Eden, there was an open heaven. As Adam and Eve walked with God, it seemed as if there was no division between heaven and earth. In particular, there was a close relationship between the natural Zion, which is Jerusalem, and spiritual Zion. In Hebrews 12, the writer reminds us that **"You have come to Mount Zion, to the heavenly Jerusalem, the city of the living God."** The reference here is to a spiritual Zion. Most believers in Replacement Theology have limited themselves to thinking of Zion, Israel and the new Jerusalem in spiritualized terms. Secular or natural Zionists, on the other hand, talk only about a physical, natural Zion. However, if we want to understand and interpret the Scriptures in their full context, we need to understand that God's purposes for world redemption include both the physical, natural Zion as well as the spiritual Zion. What happens to the actual land of Israel is of vital importance to the fulfillment of the plans for the redemption of the whole world.

We live in days of restoration when we are seeing the fulfillment of many of the prophecies of the Word of God. The fulfillment of all things will include a natural and a spiritual component. An example to confirm this principle, is the rate of salvations worldwide since the dawn of modern times. Studies show that 95 percent of all the people who have been saved in the history of the world have come to know God in the past 50 years—since Israel became a nation. Almost half of the Jewish people in the world live in Israel. We cannot replace a physical Zion with a spiritual Zion, because God's plans for world redemption include both. In the past 50 years, we have seen the rebirth of the Jewish state and have witnessed its growth into an economically strong country. To say that God's plan for world redemption does not include this physical country is to take issue with the way God has chosen to fulfill His plans and accomplish His purposes on the earth.

Another one of God's purposes that must be interpreted in light of the principle, first the natural than the spiritual, is *aliyah*, or the return of the Jews to Israel. God's Word says that He will gather His people from the four corners of the earth. Although we have seen one million people return to Israel from the former Soviet Union in the last ten years, there are many more Jews in other countries of the world who have yet to return. The return of the Jews must take place in a physical manner; real people returning to a real place. Once they have come up to the physical Zion, coming up to the spiritual Zion will follow. Those who understand this truth will work to make *aliyah* possible, through prayer and specific efforts, in order to participate in the purposes of God.

This principle, first the natural then the spiritual, in regard to Israel began to be realized at the end of the 19th century. Jews began to return to their homeland to escape the harsh treatment of Tsarist Russia. In that same time period, Theodore Herzl had a vision of a Jewish state. In 1898, he convened the first Zionist conference in Basel, Switzerland. Herzl said that a Jewish state would be born within 50 years. Exactly 50 years later, in 1948, Israel was born. This did not happen without fierce opposition. Because the land, known then as Palestine, was in dispute, many people advocated turning the African nation of Uganda into the Jewish homeland, but Herzl and others insisted that their homeland needed to be that same land inhabited by the patriarchs and prophets before them. One year later, in 1899, Yeshua Messiah revealed Himself on the Mount of Olives to Joseph Rabinowitz, a Jewish rabbi from Kishinev, Moldovia. This rabbi became known as the Theodore Herzl of the Messianic Jewish movement as more Jews began to receive Yeshua as Messiah.

At the same time as this movement towards the establishment of Israel was occurring in the Middle East, the Holy Spirit was active in other parts of the world as well. On New Year's Eve 1901, at the beginning of the 20th century, the Holy Spirit was poured out in Topeka, Kansas. The outpouring of the Holy Spirit at Topeka ignited a worldwide move of the Spirit and is considered to be the birth of Pentecostalism. The presence of God was very powerful, and people started to speak in other tongues. In January 2000, *Life* magazine listed the Topeka event as one of the most significant dates of the last 2000 years. Today there are over 500 million Pentecostals worldwide. Consequently, the 20th century became known as the Century of the Holy Spirit. Just as God acted in the natural, preparing the way for Israel to become a nation, He acted in the spiritual world, and began to pour out His Spirit on all flesh.

The relationship between what happens to Israel and the move of the Spirit of God continued throughout the century. David du Plessis, known as "Mr. Pentecost," was declared by *Time* magazine to be one of the most influential Christian leaders of the 20th century. God used him to take the message of the Holy Spirit to Catholic as well as Protestant leaders. He was used as a catalyst to bring about unity among the Body of Christ. Du Plessis had a very strong understanding of the place of Israel. From Joel 3, the Lord showed him that He would pour out His Spirit on all flesh after Israel was restored as a nation.

In 1948, some time after this revelation, he was in a car accident. As he lay in the hospital, seeking the Lord about what had happened to him, the Lord told him that he (David) needs to be broken before He could use him. Not too long after that, while still in hospital, Du Plessis heard on the radio that Israel had become a nation. God immediately healed him, and he went on to lead hundreds of thousands of people into the fullness of the Holy Spirit around the world. At the same time, many powerful men of God (including Billy Graham and Oral Roberts) were emerging. The Latter Rain movement began in Canada, with the restoration of free worship in the spirit.

Another watershed year was 1967, pointing out the parallel between world events in the natural and the works of God in the spiritual. Although Israel had been independent for almost 20 years, its capital, Jerusalem, still remained in Arab hands. But in June of 1967, Israeli paratroopers liberated East Jerusalem and the Old City, restoring Jerusalem once again as a united city. For the first time in centuries, Jews were able to pray freely and without fear at the Western Wall. Even as this miraculous event took place in Israel, the Spirit of God was poured out over the Church. In 1967, at Duquesne University, God opened up a fountain of the Holy Spirit upon a prayer gathering of Roman Catholics, and the Catholic Charismatic movement was born. It is said that even the Pope was praying for a new Pentecost, and that is in effect what happened. Over 100 million Catholics have received the baptism of the Holy Spirit since that time, and it is safe to say that it was no accident that this occurred in the same year as the city of Jerusalem was returned in its entirety to the Jews.

For the Catholics, the timing of the two events was particularly symbolic. In the past, the Catholics had always believed that "all roads led to Rome," and that the decisions made by the Pope carried as much, if not more, authority than Scripture. The outpouring of the Holy Spirit upon the Catholic Church in 1967 was a reminder to the Catholics that all roads do not in fact lead to Rome; they lead to Jerusalem. As the Jews were praying at the Western Wall in the city of Jerusalem, the Spirit of God was moving throughout the world.

People need to understand the reality of the dynamic that the natural precedes the spiritual, for in so doing, they will become stronger partners of God's end-time purposes.

God is restoring all things—the heavenly Zion (Heb. 12) and earthly Zion (Psa. 48). Jerusalem and Israel are being built into fullness (Psa. 102) as well as being grafted back into the olive tree (Rom. 11) in preparation for Messiah's coming. When Messiah comes, He will unite the heavenly and earthly Zion. The Church and Israel will become one as all things in heaven and earth will be one in Christ Jesus (Eph. 1:10; Zech. 14:12). Until that time we need to recognize the damage done by Replacement Theology. Born-again Christians under Adolph Hitler were killing Jews because of the influence of Replacement Theology. This originated from Martin Luther. Zechariah 14:12 says that in the last days all nations will fight against the Jews and that the eyes of those who do will rot in their sockets. Their tongues will rot in their mouths and their flesh on their bodies. Pray that all churches worldwide will be delivered from this theology and stand as watchmen on the walls of Jerusalem, provoking the Jews to jealousy, not fighting against them. The apostolic-prophetic plumb line of restoration is that Jews and Gentiles are being reconciled as one, preparing the way for Messiah to be revealed.

Stone 6:
Abortion—the Second Jewish Holocaust

"You shall not kill" (Exodus 20:13).

"O God, do not keep silent; be not quiet, O God, be not still. See how our enemies are astir, how your foes rear their heads. ... 'Come,' they say, 'let us destroy them as a nation, that the name of Israel be remembered no more'" (Psalm 83:1-4).

Abortion is a practice that goes back to the days of the god Molech when babies were sacrificed in the Hinnom Valley outside of Jerusalem. Molech was often represented as a brass idol with outstretched hands. A fire was made under its hands. When the hands were red-hot, babies were placed in them to burn while incessant drum beats drowned the cries of anguish.

Satan has always felt threatened by the Jewish people—not because they are Jews but because their destiny, deliverance and salvation mean his doom. His strategy throughout history has been to wipe out the Jews in any way that he can, especially the babies.

The first example we see in the Bible is that of Moses, the deliverer of his people out of Egypt. Pharaoh was threatened that a deliverer would come from among the Jews, so he ordered all male Jewish babies to be killed. By this massacre of innocent blood, he thought to protect his kingdom.

The same thing occurred again at the birth of Jesus. King Herod received news that a king had been born to the Jews. He too felt threatened, just as Pharaoh did, and so he ordered all male babies killed, hoping that he would be able to kill Jesus, but Jesus fled with His parents into Egypt.

Throughout the 20th century, Satan has continued to unfold his plan of destruction. At the beginning of the century, the Jews began to return to Israel and reclaim the land that was promised to them. As the century progressed, it was clear that the Jews were moving closer to an independent country of their own. The enemy again attempted to intervene in history, this time through Adolph Hitler's diabolic plan called "The Final Solution," which called for the extermination of all Jews. One and a half million children were killed in the Holocaust to try to abort God's purposes to bring about the rebirth of Israel and the deliverance of the Jewish people. Unfortunately, this was not the last time that the survival of innocent Jewish babies was challenged.

When Satan realized that he could not wipe out the Jewish people through the Holocaust, he tried another demonic strategy: abortion. While the Jewish people say that the Holocaust will not happen again, another holocaust has and is actually occurring among the Jews, one I call the Second Jewish Holocaust. *It is estimated that over 6,000,000 Jewish babies worldwide have been aborted in the second half of the 20th century since Hitler's Holocaust.* Unfortunately, possibly the highest percentage of babies of any race group to be killed by abortion is among the Jews. I do not believe that this is an accident. It is a demonic strategy of Satan. When you combine the total number of murders from Hitler's Holocaust and from the holocaust of abortion, you reach close to 12 million people, which is the number of Jews living in the world today. There is nothing we can do about Hitler's Holocaust. It is part of history. But the holocaust of abortion is still being perpetrated.

The Jewish people say the holocaust will never be repeated, but it is in fact happening again! Abortion was legalized in Israel in 1976, only three years after it was legalized in the United States. The United States has greatly influenced Israel in this. Pray for legalized abortion to be removed especially from the United States, Russia, France and Israel so that this second holocaust may be stopped.

Abortion in Israel

There are between 60,000 and 80,000 abortions in Israel each year, of which the majority are considered legal abortions. The most common reasons for legal abortions in Israel are pregnancies among single mothers, women over 40, danger to the life of the mother, and medical problems detected in the fetus.

Abortion in Israel is used as a convenient method of birth control. A young unmarried girl still living at home needs her parents' consent to receive an aspirin but is able to receive an abortion in secret. A medical committee makes the decision; fathers of the unborn babies, husbands and parents are not required to be notified.

Married women over age 35 account for over 50 percent of abortions. These women usually have older children, have begun to reclaim some of their independence, and did not anticipate a late pregnancy. Frequently, family finances are already stretched to the limit. They are not willing to accept the demanding physical, financial and emotional responsibility of caring for an infant, and choose to abort.

Military service is mandatory for all Israelis over the age of 18, both men and women. When young women join the army, sexual activity is an assumption and they are automatically authorized two free abortions during their military service. If a young woman becomes pregnant and chooses to keep her baby, she is discharged from the army. Fewer than one percent of all abortions in Israel occur because of incest or rape.

Abortion Among Jews Worldwide

It is also interesting that the abortion rate is very high also among Jewish people in Russia, France, United States and Great Britain—the countries where there are large Jewish populations. In Russia, many Jewish women have five to ten abortions as a form of birth control. In France, where the abortion pill was developed, the abortion rate is very high. In the United States and England, many pro-choice and feminist groups are led by secular Jews.

Removing the Stone

1.   *Pray for a Joshua Generation:* We must pray for a revival of righteous moral standards and revelation to come to this generation of Jewish young people. We need to pray that they would stand against this Second Jewish Holocaust and say, "Enough! This has to stop!" We need to pray that they would rise up as a Joshua generation; a moral vanguard against the tide of iniquity and unrighteousness of their time.

2.   *Pray for Jewish Doctors and Medical Professionals:* We must unite in prayer for the Jewish doctors and medical professionals, interceding that they would follow the example of Dr. Bernard Nathanson, a Jewish physician once known as the "Abortion King" who admitted to performing over 75,000 abortions but who received a divine revelation about the sanctity of human life beginning at conception. Dr. Nathanson is now a vocal leader of the pro-life movement in the United States.

3.   *Pray for Understanding:* We must pray that the truth of life beginning at conception and the horrible reality of abortion be revealed to the Jewish people worldwide. We must pray that they choose life rather than death for future generations.

4.   *Pray for the Jewish Leadership:* We must pray for the rabbis, politicians and other Jewish leaders who influence the legal and social systems. We must pray that they take this second holocaust more seriously and end it before millions more Jewish babies are killed. We must pray that these leaders heed the words of the Babylonian Talmud Sanhedrin 37, in Mishna 20:

> **"For this reason was man created alone, to teach them that whosoever destroys a single soul of Israel, scripture imputes [guilt] to him as though he had destroyed a complete world, and whosoever preserves a single soul of Israel, scripture ascribes merit to him as though he had preserved a complete world."**

Abortion has been a terrible sin among the Gentiles throughout the world. It is possible to make a connection between the abortion rate in a country and the level of revival happening there. Latin America, where abortions are illegal in most countries, is experiencing very deep and strong revival in many locations. On the other hand, the occurrences of revival in Western Europe, where abortions are legal and commonplace, is extremely low. Most Jews outside Israel live in countries where the abortion rate is very high. In Israel the policy regarding abortion is largely affected by Europe and the United States, and not by the Arab nations where abortion among Jewish populations is much lower.

We know that God hates the shedding of innocent blood. We pray that the Lord Himself would intervene to bring an end to this holocaust of abortion among the Jewish people, the apple of His eye, before the other half of the Jews left in the world perish. We pray that God, in His mercy, will open a fountain over Israel and the Jewish people worldwide. We pray that the revival, so clearly prophesied by the prophets, would come to Israel and all Jewish people. Pray that this second holocaust will end, that Jewish babies will be born, and that the Jewish people will be born-again. Consequently God's peace will come to Jerusalem.

Stone 7:
The Fullness of the Gentiles

"I do not want you to be ignorant of this mystery, brothers, so that you may not be conceited: Israel has experienced a hardening in part until the full number of the Gentiles has come in. And so all Israel will be saved, as it is written:

'The deliverer will come from Zion; he will turn godlessness away from Jacob. And this is my covenant with them when I take away their sins'" (Romans 11:25-27).

Abraham's Descendants

God's original intent in creating man was so that we might know and enjoy Him forever. Unfortunately Adam, the first man, failed to fulfill this basic intention, and his descendants followed suit. Even Noah, who is described in Genesis as "a just man, perfect in his ways," was not able to restore the original relationship that God had intended for man to have with Him.

God chose a man called Abraham (at the time of his calling he was known as Abram) to begin His plan of salvation by setting apart a people that He would call by His name. Abraham was from a city called Ur, in what is today known as Iraq, a Gentile civilization. Because of Abraham's faith and his obedience to God, this was credited to him as righteousness and he was known as a friend of God. God called him out of his homeland, brought him to a foreign land, and promised to make him a father of many nations.

Abraham's natural sons, Ishmael and Isaac and their descendants, also failed in their divine calling to know God and enjoy Him forever. Israel was called to be a light to the nations, yet Jesus tells us that because they missed the hour of their visitation, God put blinders over their eyes. They missed the Messiah when He walked among them. As a result of their failure, the Gospel has gone out of Jerusalem to the whole world. Hundreds of thousands of Jews received Jesus in the first century. Since the expulsion of the Jews from Jerusalem, the Gospel has gone out to millions of Gentiles around the world.

The Time of the Gentiles

When His disciples asked him about the end of the age, Jesus told them a parable:

> "Look at the fig tree and all the trees. When they sprout leaves, you can see for yourselves and know that summer is near. Even so, when you see these things happening, you know that the kingdom of God is near... Jerusalem will be trampled on by the Gentiles until the times of the Gentiles are fulfilled" (Luke 21:29-31,34).

Throughout the Bible, the fig tree symbolizes Israel. The Lord told us that when the fig tree and all the other trees blossom, the end is near. Blossoming means that the tree is bursting into flower because the dormant time of winter is over. Springtime represents the fulfillment of promise.

In 1967, three events took place to indicate the approach of the end times: God opened a fountain upon the Jews and Jews started to come to faith in Jesus. For the first time in history, Jerusalem came under Jewish rule and became the capital of Israel. Just as the wall in Berlin later came down, so did the Old CIty walls in Jerusalem during Israel's Six-Day War. As the Jewish people flocked to the Wailing Wall to pray, God began to pour out His Spirit and reveal the Messiah to them. God also unleashed a mighty move of His Holy Spirit upon the Catholic Church and the Catholic Charismatic movement was born.

At that time, there were barely 100 native Israeli believers in Israel and a few thousand worldwide. In the year 2000, there were approximately 300,000 Messianic believers in Israel and the world combined. Some say that the number may be even greater. These believers are blossoms on the fig tree, a fulfillment of God's promise. They are like a small breeze beginning to build which will climax in a strong wind completely lifting the veil off the eyes of Israel as they come to their Messiah, mourning for the one whom they have pierced (Zech. 12:10). It is estimated that more Gentiles have received the Messiah since 1967 than in all history since the time of Jesus' birth. As the wave of the salvation of Gentiles reaches its peak and the wild olive branches are fully grafted into the olive tree, the natural olive branches (the Jews) will also be fully grafted back onto their own olive tree. According to Luke 21:32, this generation (since 1967) will not pass until this promise is fulfilled.

Jesus also says,

"And this gospel of the kingdom will be preached in the whole world as a testimony to all nations, and then the end will come" (Matthew 24:14).

We know that Jesus is coming back when the Gospel of the kingdom is preached to all the nations of the world. At this time in history, there are no nations where people have not heard the Gospel. The Word of God is going forth in nations where, in 1967, there were virtually no believers. These include Mongolia, Libya, Afghanistan, Kazakhstan, Kyrgyzstan, Tajikistan, Turkmenistan, Uzbekistan, Maldives, Comoro Islands, Tunisia, Qatar, Yemen, Albania, Morocco, Somalia, Saudi Arabia and all other Arab nations and even Israel.

The word *ethnos* in Greek does not just refer to the larger nations of the world. It includes people, language and culture groups. There are approximately 10,000 such groups where a local church is not planted. The end will come when there is a witness of the Gospel established in each 'nation' of the world. According to Romans 11, quoted at the beginning of this section, as the fullness of the Gentiles comes in, more of the blindness will be removed from Israel and Israel will be saved.

It is important for Christians to remember that every time they preach the Gospel around them, they are praying for the peace of Jerusalem. Why? Because peace will not come to Jerusalem until the fullness of the Gentiles has come in. Each time a Gentile accepts Jesus as his or her Messiah, the Kingdom of God and the return of Jesus gets one step closer.

The book of Isaiah is full of descriptions of the Messiah. I find it very interesting that the Dead Sea Scrolls were discovered by a Gentile, a Bedouin shepherd boy. God used a Gentile to give us the book of Isaiah, preserved almost in its entirety. The book of Isaiah proves that the idea of a Redeemer, a Saviour, a Messiah (which means "anointed one" in Hebrew), is not a New Covenant concept and that Christians were not the first to think of it. Jews and Gentiles alike need to understand that the promise of Messiah is rooted in the *Tanach*, the Hebrew Scriptures, and finds its fulfillment in the life, teachings, death and resurrection of Jesus as recorded in the New Covenant. Even at this writing, vast numbers of Christians around the world are beginning to rediscover their biblical Jewish roots by studying the *Tanach*, observing the biblical feasts, and asking the Lord for a greater revelation of His purposes.

The climax to bring peace to Jerusalem will be the return of the Messiah. When He returns, He will place His feet upon the Mount of Olives and take His rightful place on the throne of David. The prophet Ezekiel describes this moment:

> "He said, 'Son of Man, this is the place of my throne and the place for the soles of my feet. This is where I will live among the Israelites forever'" (Ezekiel 43:7).

When He comes, Jesus will not only be King of Israel but of all nations. Beyond the shadow of any doubt, this will be the most awesome event in the history of the universe. Imagine a situation where not just regional, but international pandemonium and chaos come under the dominion of God, who will exercise His dominion and reign to bring order back to this planet.

This is why it is imperative for Christians everywhere to pray for the peace of Jerusalem. It is not just an insignificant small city in a small country in the Middle East. Jerusalem is a city of international and eternal significance. Isaiah tells us that in the last days, the Lord's temple will be raised as chief among the mountains. It will be raised above the hills and all nations will stream into it. The Law will go forth from Zion and the Word of the Lord from Jerusalem (Isa. 2:1-3).

All Nations Convocations

Jesus, who was born, lived and died as a Jew, quoted from the Hebrew Scriptures when he said, "My house will be called a house of prayer for all nations" (Matthew 21:13; Isaiah 56:7-8). In 1987, when the Lord called me to Jerusalem, He called me to pray primarily for the Jewish people. He gave the name of the ministry, Jerusalem House of Prayer for All Nations, and called us to start 24-hour worship and intercession for Israel and the nations. We established the ministry on the Mount of Olives where Jesus, the King of the Jews, did not pray that the Kingdom of God would come only to Israel but that the Kingdom of God would come "on earth, as it is in heaven." He proclaimed the Kingdom of God over all the nations. In addition to praying for *aliyah* and for the salvation of Israel, the Lord called us to pray for all the nations of the world and for the salvation of the people from all nations. We recognized that, as people are proclaiming the Gospel to and praying for the salvation of neighbors, friends and family members, they are in fact actively praying for the peace of Jerusalem. Peace will not come to the nations until the fullness of the Gentiles comes in from every nation.

In addition to praying for the salvation of people from the nations, God has called us to mobilize leaders to pray for the salvation of the nations. In 1994, we convened the first All Nations Convocation in Jerusalem, for the purpose of praying for the peace of Jerusalem, *aliyah* and the reconciliation of Jews, Arabs and all nations in Messiah. At this convocation, we presented prayer needs from every nation in the world and the primary focus of our prayers was for the removal of the stones that hinder the fullness of the Gentiles coming into the Kingdom of God and His cultivated olive tree. Two hundred leaders from 140 nations were represented at this convocation. We have continued these convocations every two years, throughout the 1990s. In 1996, 400 leaders from 180 nations attended; and in 1998, there were 800 leaders from about 200 nations. In the year 2000, we had more than 2,000 delegates from over 200 nations.

One of the primary focuses remains prayer for the stones to be removed and the fullness of the Gentiles to come in from every language, nation and people group (*ethnos*). At the All Nations Convocation Jerusalem 2000, Dr. Luis Bush helped us pray for the 500 remaining *ethnos*/people groups in all the nations in the world that still do not have a church planting team to bring the Gospel to them. We also prayed for church planting teams to be sent into every one of these people groups and all the nations where they are, that the Gospel may penetrate every people group on earth. We know that the salvation of Israel will be fully released when the fullness of the Gentiles comes in. We are encouraged to know almost as many Gentiles have received the Lord in the last few decades as have in the last 2,000 years of the history of the Church. The God of the breakthrough is breaking into every nation to establish His Kingdom.

Keep praying for the fullness of the Gentiles to come in from every nation and every *ethnos*, preparing the way for the fullness of the salvation of Israel.

Stone 8:
Salvation of the Jewish People

"I am not ashamed of the Gospel, because it is the power of God for the salvation of everyone who believes: first for the Jew, then for the Gentile" (Romans 1:16).

"Oh, that salvation for Israel would come out of Zion! When the LORD restores the fortunes of his people, let Jacob rejoice and Israel be glad!" (Psalm 14:7).

The Messianic Jewish movement began with Jesus in a big way in the first century. Almost all the apostles except Luke were Jewish. They turned Jerusalem and the world upside down and became a light to the nations as Jesus prophesied. Today, over two billion people claim to be Christians— branches grafted into the olive tree. After the split between Jewish and Gentile believers in the second century, the Messianic Jewish movement has continued to be alive in a very small way through the next 1,600 years. In 1842 Michael Solomon Alexander became the first Jewish bishop in Jerusalem in over 1,700 years, serving in Christ Church. Again Jews began receiving their Messiah in a progressive way. In 1899—one year after Theodore Herzl called the Zionist Congress in 1898 in Basel, Switzerland, and prophesied Israel would be born in exactly 50 years—Joseph Rabinowitz, a rabbi from Kishnev, Moldovia, was visited on the Mount of Olives by Yeshua, who revealed Himself to him as the Messiah. This began the restoration of the Messianic Jewish movement at the turn of the 1900s. Rabinowitz is known as the father of the Messianic Jewish movement.

The salvation of the Jewish people is a most significant topic, especially as we understand the events that will mark the end times and herald the second coming of the Messiah. Salvation began and will culminate with the Jews. From the beginning to the end of history, all things are centered in Jesus. God accepted even Abel's blood sacrifice because it pointed the way to Messiah. The same is true of the sacrifices that were offered up by Abraham, those in the days of the prophets and until the time of Jesus Himself. The lamb's blood spread on the doorposts of the Israelites' homes in Egypt, protecting them from the Angel of Death, was a forerunner of the blood of Jesus, the ultimate sacrificial Lamb, whose blood saves us from eternal death.

Christians worldwide believe that Jesus is the Son of David and the Messiah. Jewish people generally believe that the coming Messiah will be the Son of David. There are growing numbers of Christians in the world who believe, and rightly so, that Jews who receive Jesus as their Messiah should not "convert" to Christianity nor call themselves "Christians." Rather, these people should maintain their Jewish identities. Jesus Himself lived as an observant Jew all of His life. It was not until the third century, when Christianity became the official religion of the Holy Roman Empire, that Jews who accepted Jesus as their Messiah were actually forbidden to maintain ties to their Jewish roots. Interestingly enough, it is the Gentiles, the wild olive branches that are grafted into the cultivated olive tree of the commonwealth of Israel. Jews who come to faith in Jesus are not required to change their faith in the same way. For all of God's people, Jew and Gentile alike, our common root is in the root of David.

In the coming years or decades, or until the Messiah returns, millions of Jewish people will receive their Messiah. In this, they are preparing the way for Jesus' return as they say, "Blessed is he that comes in the name of the Lord." From this, it appears that the lack of salvation of the Jews is the final stone that needs to be removed as we pray for the peace of Jerusalem and the fulfillment of God's purposes.

Just as a stone was rolled away from the opening of the tomb at Jesus' resurrection, so will a stone be removed from heaven to prepare the way for the Messiah to come. No one knows when this will happen, not even Jesus Himself. This stone will be removed as God moves upon the Jewish people to remove the blinders from their eyes—to a large extent in response to the proclamation of the Gospel, and the prayers and praises of Christians all over the world. These prayers of intercession will pierce the darkness of oppression upon the Jews. The breakthrough of intercessory prayer will rend the heavens and produce an outpouring of the Holy Spirit upon the Jews. Gentile believers will increasingly become light and salt to the Jews in their midst, providing comfort in the midst of persecution.

The entire New Covenant is the testimony of Jesus' death for the salvation of all people—Gentiles and Jews alike. Israel was created to be a light to the nations. Jesus is the Light of the World. Salvation is truly of the Jews. It was the Jews who first took the Gospel to the nations. It is estimated that by the end of the year 2000, there will be over two billion Christians worldwide.

Of the Jews, scripture tells us, **"He came to that which was His own, but His own did not receive Him" (John 1:11).** Jesus said that because they did not receive Him, the Jews missed the hour of their visitation. In Luke 19:41-44, Jesus weeps over Jerusalem:

> **"As he approached Jerusalem and saw the city, he wept over it and said, 'If you, even you, had only known on this day what would bring you peace—but now it is hidden from your eyes. The days will come upon you when your enemies will build an embankment against you and encircle you and hem you in on every side. They will dash you to the ground, you and the children within your walls. They will not leave one stone on another, because you did not recognize the time of God's coming to you.'"**

Jerusalem was destroyed just as Jesus prophesied. With the scattering of the Jewish people, the Gospel went to the Gentiles. By the end of the third century, there were very few Jewish believers and the situation remained so until the 20th century. Many Jews formally converted to Christianity because of laws which forbade those who accepted Jesus to continue practicing the Jewish traditions.

Even as the 20th century ushered in the return of the Jews to Palestine (later to become Israel), it also ushered in the salvation of the Jewish people, as Joseph Rabinowitz, the spiritual father of the Messianic Jewish movement, received salvation on the Mount of Olives in Jerusalem in 1899. When Israel became a state in 1948, there were only a few thousand Messianic Jews in the world. Today the number is approximately 300,000. So we see that the fig tree has started blossoming, especially since the reunification of Jerusalem in 1967 when God started to open a fountain on the Jewish people. We believe that there will be an even greater fountain opened over them in Jerusalem and all Israel and all nations in the early years and decades of the third millennium.

The prophet Zechariah illustrates this promise:

> "And I will pour out on the house of David and on the inhabitants of Jerusalem a spirit of grace and supplication. They will look on me, the one they have pierced, and they will mourn for him as one mourns for an only child, and grieve bitterly for him as one grieves for a firstborn son. On that day a fountain will be opened to the house of David and the inhabitants of Jerusalem, to cleanse them from sin and impurity" (Zechariah 12:10–13:1).

We know that the blossoming of the fig tree indicates that summer is near. When the fig tree blossoms, Jesus will come back; it indicates that the end is near.

Keys to the Salvation of Israel

1. *Repentance and Forgiveness from the Gentile Church:* It is estimated that one half, or more, of Jews and Arabs who receive Jesus in these days do so because the Lord reveals Himself to them in visions, dreams and supernatural revelations. Mostly, this is because the face of Jesus has been drastically misrepresented to the Jewish people and people throughout the Middle East by the terrible sins of the Church throughout its history. The Inquisition, the Crusades (killing Arabs and Jews alike) and the Holocaust are atrocious, shameful instances of the Gentiles wanting to assert themselves over Jews and Arabs.

   One of the keys to the salvation of the Jewish people is for repentance by and forgiveness of the Gentile Church for its terrible sins committed in history. There are indications that this is already beginning to happen through prayer conferences, reconciliation walks and conferences, as many Christians from around the world start to reject deception. Christians are rediscovering the Jewish roots of their faith, celebrating the Jewish biblical feasts of *Rosh*

Hashanah (Day of Trumpets/New Year), *Yom Kippur* (Day of Atonement), *Shavuot* (Pentecost), *Pessach* (Passover) and *Succot* (Feast of Tabernacles). As we live in the days of restoration, we shall surely see the Gentile Church united as one in the cultivated olive tree with the natural branches, the Jewish believers.

2. *Intercession:* Christians must take up the role of watchmen, standing in the gap and praying for the salvation of the Jewish people. Joseph's brothers recognized him at the appointed time, after the Egyptian king had honored him, many years after they had sold him into slavery. Christians must pray that the same thing will happen again, that Jesus' brothers, the Jews, will recognize Him as their long awaited Messiah, as their Brother and their Lord. Pray that congregations will be planted in all the 80 or more cities of Israel, preparing the way for Messiah's coming. He said we would not finish going through all the cities of Israel before the Son of Man comes. Stand as watchmen on your gates of the World Wide Watch, as part of the wall of fire around Jerusalem.

3. *Comfort the Jewish People:* God exhorts believers to "**Comfort, comfort my people,...**" **(Isaiah 40:1)**. Christians must continue to stand for God's purposes for the Jewish people. They must increase their support through friendship, acts of kindness, blessing, encouragement and sharing the love and salvation of God that is available to them. They can encourage their Jewish friends who are thinking of making *aliyah*, and share the way of peace with them and also with those who live in the land, both Jews and Arabs. These ongoing acts of mercy will contribute to paving the way for God to bring Jew and Gentile together as one in Messiah.

4. *Identificational Repentance by Jewish believers:* In Daniel 9, the prophet Daniel begs forgiveness for the sins of his people, identifying with them and repenting for them. Jewish believers need to follow this example and stand in identificational repentance for the sins of their people. Even as the Romans were guilty of killing Jesus, the Jews were also guilty, for they said that Jesus should be crucified. They cried, "**Let his blood be upon us and on our children**" (Matt. 27:

25). Identificational repentance is one of the keys to the salvation of Israel. Jewish believers are in many ways identifying with the sins of their people and saying we have sinned, we have rebelled, we have acted wickedly (Dan. 9; Psa. 14:7). In Psalm 80, the psalmist declares three times, **"Restore us, O God Almighty, make your face shine upon us, that we may be saved."** This is beginning to happen in increasing ways in Israel, and it is led by local believers.

5.   *Lifting the Veil:* We pray that God, at His sovereign appointed time, will remove the veil He put over the eyes of the Jewish people when they missed the hour of their visitation. We pray that God will visit them again with a divine revelation from heaven. We know that the latter rain is greater than the early rain, and we pray for all Israel to be saved. We seek the fulfillment of God's calling, purpose and destiny for Israel to be a light to the nations, culminating in Messiah's return and the restoration of all things in heaven and earth, one in Christ Jesus.

We know that even as Israel was born in a day in the natural, and that 3,000 were born in a day in the Spirit (on Pentecost), we know too that God is going to progressively lift the veil from the eyes of Israel. We pray that they may be saved and corporately say **"Blessed is he who comes in the name of the Lord."** This will remove the stone of unbelief and release Messiah from the heavens to take up His throne in Jerusalem.

Stone 9:
The Bride Making Herself Ready

"Then the angel said to me, 'Write, "Blessed are those who are invited to the wedding supper of the Lamb!"' And he added, 'These are the true words of God'" (Revelation 19:9).

Praying for the peace of Jerusalem involves much more than focusing our thoughts, prayers and intercession on the return of the Jews, Jerusalem and the chaotic events of the Middle East. Praying for the peace of Jerusalem also requires an intense time of personal preparation. We know that Yeshua is waiting for His bride, and that He will return when the bride is ready.

The Lord Yeshua, King and Bridegroom, has been waiting a long time for His bride. I believe He was already thinking of His eternal wedding when He turned the water into wine 2,000 years ago at Cana. If you are single, wanting to be married and getting impatient, talk to Jesus. He has been waiting 2,000 years for His wedding. And whether you are single or married, do not miss out on the big wedding that will last for all eternity!

Some people believe that we are waiting for Jesus to come before they get ready for the wedding. He has been ready and waiting all the time. The wedding will take place as soon as the bride makes herself ready.

As Revelation 19 says, this wedding will take place at the time that He condemns the great prostitute who corrupted the earth by her adulteries. True and just are the judgments of the Lord. The time of the wedding will be a time of rejoicing, gladness and giving glory to God.

God uses a wide variety of things to prepare us for the wedding, starting with Yeshua Himself. He has given us the Holy Spirit, fire, trials and persecutions. Our degree of readiness for the wedding feast of the Lamb is often determined by our response to the trials we experience. We become ready by yielding to God and His direction. We must be sure that we have oil in our lamps by confessing our sins every day and being filled afresh each morning by the Holy Spirit. We must make sure that we are vigilant and wise virgins with oil in our lamps and not sleeping, drowsy or foolish virgins without any oil in their lamps.

"At midnight the cry rang out: 'Here's the bridegroom! Come out to meet him!' Then all the virgins woke up and trimmed their lamps. The foolish ones said to the wise, 'Give us some of your oil; our lamps are going out.' 'No,' they replied, 'there may not be enough for both us and you. Instead, go to those who sell oil and buy some for yourselves.' But while they were on their way to buy the oil, the bridegroom arrived. The virgins who were ready went in with him to the wedding banquet. And the door was shut. Later the others also came. 'Sir! Sir!' they said. 'Open the door for us!' But he replied, 'I tell you the truth, I do not know you'" (Matthew 25:6-12).

Fine, bright, clean and white linen will be given to the bride to wear, representing the righteous acts of the saints (Rev. 19:8). Ultimately, however, intimacy with Jesus, and not our work for Him, is the most important factor in these last days. Doing good work for Jesus is not a replacement for intimacy with him. Safeguard your intimacy with Jesus and allow him to do His good works through you.

A Personal Passion for Jesus

In these last days, it is of the greatest importance that we not allow our love for Jesus to grow cold. In Matthew 24:12 we read that, because of the increase of wickedness and lawlessness, the love of many will grow cold. The Lord wants the fire of our love for Him to be kindled and burn like an eternal flame, and He wants us to be consumed by a passion to live and die for Him. If we are passionately in love with Jesus, our love will not grow cold. Instead, it will burn like a red-hot fire, and warm all those who come near us.

We must understand that God has purposed that all of our life should be worshipful and spiritual. We should not separate the secular and the spiritual. We should have passion for Jesus in all we do. Brother Lawrence said every pancake he flipped and every straw he picked up, he did for the glory of God.

In spite of the difficulties we face in sustaining our passion for Jesus in a society ridden with distractions, we simply have to spend quality time in communion with Jesus through the Holy Spirit if we are to keep the fire burning. In the midst of our busy lives, we must guard this time with Him jealously, even as our Lord jealously desires our fellowship, faithfulness and love.

> "You adulterous people, don't you know that friendship with the world is hatred toward God? Anyone who chooses to be a friend of the world becomes an enemy of God. Or do you think Scripture say without reason that the Spirit he caused to live in us envies intensely?" (James 4:4-5)

The essence of wickedness that causes our love to grow cold is idolatry, which means putting anyone or anything else before the Lord in our lives. If we are passionately in love with Jesus, who is the Truth incarnate, we will not be deceived.

The Land Married to the Lord

> "No longer will they call you Deserted, or name your land Desolate. But you will be called Hephzibah [in Hebrew, 'My delight is in her'], and your land Beulah [in Hebrew, 'married']; for the Lord will take delight in you and your land will be married" (Isaiah 62:4).

Traditionally, we think of the wedding supper of the Lamb as the fulfillment of the purposes of God for His creation. We understand that His bride is His Church, and all who believe in Yeshua will be part of that final and eternal celebration. The prophet Isaiah talks about the land actually being married. Who would the land be married to if not the Lord. Imagine—Yeshua will be married to the land of Israel. The following verses describe the delight the Lord takes in His land:

> "The Gentiles shall see your righteousness and all the kings your glory. You shall be called by a new name, which the mouth of the LORD will name. You shall be a crown of glory in the hand of the LORD, and a royal diadem in the hand of your God" (Isaiah 62:2-3).

Truly, this sounds like the description of a proud bridegroom boasting about His bride!

The people of God, His Church, will be married to the Lord. His land—all that Jerusalem represents from the Nile to the Euphrates—that He promised to the descendants of Abraham, will also be married to the Lord. In the section on Replacement Theology, we discussed that natural events often precede and mirror events that are taking place in the spiritual realm. It is as if much of life takes place on two separate plains. But at the end of time, when all of God's purposes will have been fulfilled, there will be a great harmony between the natural and the spiritual. The two will come together as Yeshua marries His land, His Jewish people and His Church.

> "I have posted watchmen on your walls, O Jerusalem; they will never be silent day or night. You who call on the Lord, give yourselves no rest, and give him no rest till he establishes Jerusalem and makes her the praise of the earth" (Isaiah 62:7).

These verses about the watchmen on the walls of Jerusalem are well known to all of our community and have become foundational verses in the prayer watches that have been set up around the world. The verses reveal the heart of God. It is interesting to note that these verses come after the verses that talk about the land being married to the Lord. Verse 5 is a link between the two, for it says, **"As a young man marries a maiden, so will your sons marry you; as a bridegroom rejoices over his bride, so will your God rejoice over you."** Yeshua wants to find a bride for Himself. This is why God is taking no rest. He longs to take a bride for Himself that is splendid and radiant, and He will not rest until He does. We need to accept this challenge, giving ourselves no rest until we see that the bride is prepared and worthy of the Bridegroom.

Watching for the Lord

To watch something is to pay close attention to it. We watch things that we are concerned about or that we care about. To look at something is to look at it casually. Synonyms for the verb 'watch' include to observe, to expect, to await and to guard. The verb 'watch' connotes action, attentiveness and vigilance. It is not passive. Watching for the Lord involves our whole being.

Watching the Lord—observing Him, waiting for Him, listening to Him—is very exciting. God created us to watch Him. In Revelation 1:14,16 we read that His face is like the sun shining in all of its strength; His eyes are like blazing fire. God wants us to look into His face and to behold Him. As we behold Him in the Spirit, we are changed into His likeness from glory to glory. Watching the Lord is one of the most important things we can do.

The Lord is altogether lovely and wonderful to watch. Paul tells us that we should dwell, think or concentrate on the following words describing the Lord, and dwell upon Him:

> "**Whatever is true, whatever is noble, whatever is right, whatever is pure, whatever is lovely, whatever is admirable—if anything is excellent or praiseworthy—think about such things**" (**Philippians 4:8**).

As we approach the day of the second coming of our Lord, our focus needs to be on Him more than ever before. God wants us to hold fast to our first love. In fact, if we have lost any part of our first love, He wants it to be restored. He wants us to be watching Him continuously. Then He will instruct us and teach us in the way we should go and guide us with His eye (Psalm 32:8).

Watching, Not Worrying

Luke 12:22-40 shows us an interesting relationship between 'worrying' and 'watching.' In the first verse of this passage, Jesus instructs His disciples, "Do not worry." He goes on to tells them to be watchful. There is a parallel between worrying and watching. If we are truly watching for the coming of the Lord, we are not worrying because we are confident in God's purposes. On the other hand, if we are worried about the bad things that could happen to us, we are not really watching.

"Then Jesus said to his disciples, 'Therefore I tell you, do not worry about your life, what you will eat; or about your body, what you will wear. Life is more than food, and the body more than clothes. Consider [watch] the ravens. They do not sow or reap; they have no storeroom or barn; yet God feeds them. And how much more valuable you are than birds! Who of you by worrying can add a single hour to his life? Since you cannot do this very little thing, why do you worry about the rest?

"'Consider how the lilies grow. They do not labor or spin. Yet I tell you, not even Solomon in all his splendor was dressed like one of these. If that is how God clothes the grass of the field, which is here today, and tomorrow is thrown into the fire, how much more will he clothe you, O you of little faith! And do not set your heart on what you will eat or drink; do not worry about it. For the pagan world runs after all such things, and your Father knows that you need them. But seek his kingdom, and these things will be given to you as well.

"'Do not be afraid, little flock, for your Father has been pleased to give you the kingdom. Sell your possessions and give to the poor. Provide purses for yourselves that will not wear out, a treasure in heaven that will not be exhausted, where no thief comes near and no moth destroys. For where your treasure is, there your heart will be also'" (Luke 12:22-34).

Many times in this passage, Jesus tells His disciples, "Do not worry." If we can appreciate how much God cares for the birds of the air and the lilies of the field, we will be able to understand to what extent God is able to provide for us. With this kind of total dependence on God, we will be ready for His coming. It is interesting to note that Jesus exhorts the disciples not to worry, then goes directly into the need to watch for the coming of the Lord.

"Be dressed and ready for service and keep your lamps burning, like men waiting for their master to return from a wedding banquet, so that when he comes and knocks they can immediately open the door for him. It will be good for those servants whose master finds them watching when he comes. I tell you the truth, he will dress himself to serve, will have them recline at the table, and will come and wait on them. It will be good for those servants whose master finds them ready, even if he comes in the second or third watch of the night.

But understand this: If the owner of the house had known at what hour the thief was coming, he would not have let the house be broken into. You also must be ready, because the Son of Man will come at an hour when you do not expect him" (Luke 12:35-40).

Jesus tells His disciples to be "dressed and ready for service." We need to be ready, regardless of the time—be it the middle of the day or night, summer or winter. This is one of the reasons Jesus tells us that we should not go to sleep at night without settling things with our brothers and sisters. If we allow the sun to go down on our anger and continue to nurture unresolved conflicts, and the Lord chooses that moment to return, then we will not be ready for His coming. And since we know from the very words of Jesus that He will be coming at a time we do not expect, we need to be prepared for Him at all times.

We need to put on the full armor of God each day, putting on the Lord Jesus Christ. Next, we need to be watching the Master, waiting for His return, in order to be ready for Him when He comes. Then, we should be ready to open the door as soon as He appears. We need to be at our posts at all times. As Jesus Himself says, it will be good for those servants whose master finds them watching when he comes.

Do you want to be watching when the Lord Jesus comes? If you are worrying, you are not watching. You are preoccupied with the cares of this world. But if you are not worrying, you are like the birds and lilies, trusting in Him for all of your provision. Of those whom the returning master finds watching, Jesus says, "I tell you the truth, he will dress himself to serve, will have them recline at table and will come and wait on them." As the Bridegroom, Jesus Himself will be serving the bride.

Continue praying for the peace of Jerusalem, by making yourself ready as the bride of the King of Jerusalem, because when the wedding takes place and the bride is married to the King, there will be fullness of God's goodness, glory, *shalom* (peace) and His manifest presence.

Stone 10:
The Coming of the Lord

"Look, he is coming with the clouds, and every eye will see him, even those who pierced him; and all the peoples of the earth will mourn because of him. So shall it be! Amen. I am the Alpha and the Omega,' says the Lord God, 'who is, and who was, and who is to come, the Almighty'" (Revelation 1:7-8).

Earlier, I emphasized the salvation of Israel being important to preparing the way for the King of Glory. It is the key to unlocking the heavens for the Messiah to be released to take up His throne in Jerusalem. Before Yeshua rose from the dead, the angel rolled the stone away from the tomb, preparing the way for His resurrection. As we pray and work towards all the stones being removed, we are helping to prepare the way for the coming of the Lord just as John the Baptist, Anna and Simeon prepared the way for His first coming. We are entering a *kairos* (appointed) time, a major paradigm shift as radical as the change from the Old Testament to the apostolic Church. May we be faithful to prepare the way. God is calling us to be His watchmen, the ones He desires to set upon the walls of Jerusalem to take no rest, day or night, until the way is prepared for the Father to roll away the stones from the heavens, releasing Jesus to return to earth. Jesus must remain in the heavens until the restoration of all things (Acts 3:21).

The removal of the stones means that the refreshing winds of God will finally come to Israel, creating an open heaven once again over this land and the nations. The removal of the stones will signal the restoration of all things and will announce the full restoration of Israel. Peace will finally come to Israel and to the Middle East. When the stones have been removed, the Lord will come again and take up the throne of King David.

We have now crossed over into the third millennium. In 1988 and 1989, people were writing books announcing the imminent return of Jesus and, when that did not happen, they issued statements as to why they had to revise their theories. On New Year's Eve, the last night of the 20th century, a group of intercessors and I were standing on the Mount of Olives looking over the Temple Mount and the Golden Gate. We were all hoping that the Lord might come at that moment, all the while knowing that no one knows the day nor the hour when He will come again, save the Father. It is my conviction that the Lord will come back in this generation because we are beginning to see the signs of His return everywhere.

One of the primary reasons I believe the Lord will return soon is that this generation is the "fig tree" spoken of in Luke 21:29-33. Jesus said we must look for the signs of His coming, just as we know summer is coming when the fig tree blossoms. Heaven and earth will pass away, but the words of Jesus will never pass away.

For the first time since the days of Jesus and His apostles, we can see that the fig tree is beginning to blossom. The greatest harvest that the world has ever seen is taking place among the Gentiles, and now Israel is starting to receive Messiah. Jesus said we have to watch for these things that are happening. He tells us, **"When these things begin to take place, stand up and lift up your heads, because your redemption is drawing near" (Luke 21:28).**

To truly be a watchman for the coming of the Lord means that we should be prepared for His coming. In Luke 21, Jesus tells us that we should be careful that our hearts are not weighed down with dissipation, our energies are not wasted, our attention is not scattered, and our primary attention is on the Lord. We need to remain as Mary, not Martha. Our intimacy with Jesus is even more important than ever before in these last days. We must maintain our hunger for Him; our hearts must long for His return; our souls must pant after Him even as the deer pants after water. We must guard ourselves, not be involved in "drunkenness," or excessive behavior of any kind, be it alcohol, the pursuit of pleasure, materialistic comforts or money. If our hearts are truly longing and watching for Him, our focus should be on laying up treasures in heaven that cannot be taken away instead of laying up treasures on earth. We need to know and live the scripture that says, where our treasure is, so is our heart.

We must be watchful that our hearts are not weighed down by the anxieties of life and that we learn from Jesus when He told His disciples not to worry about anything, but to trust their Master to provide their needs. Jesus says,

> **"Be always on the watch, and pray that you may be able to escape all that is about to happen, and that you may be able to stand before the Son of Man" (Luke 21:36).**

Watching for the coming of the Lord means being prepared for His coming. Be alert and pray that we may escape what is about to happen, and that we might be able to stand before Him dressed in righteousness.

The world is full of civil wars and bloodshed. There will be no peace, either in Jerusalem or in the nations of the world in a full sense, until Jesus returns. Only then will there be complete peace in Ireland, in the Middle East between the Arab nations and Israel, Europe between Bosnia and Serbia; and only then will the races of the world live in peace.

While the first-fruits are coming forth today along the highway of salvation from Egypt to Israel to Assyria, with Jews and Arabs being reconciled in Jesus the Messiah, only when Messiah returns will there fully be peace from the Nile to the Euphrates and in Jerusalem. The Garden of Eden will then be restored and Egypt, Israel and Assyria will be a blessing in the midst of the earth. This is why every believer on earth is commanded to pray for the peace of Jerusalem and for all these ten stones to be removed. Psalm 122:6 says all those who pray for her peace and love her will prosper.

Will you lead the way by raising the banner from your nation in opening a gate and highway to heaven of prayer for the peace of Jerusalem and for the highway of salvation to be fully opened between Egypt, Israel and Assyria? Will you pray for the bride from all nations to be married to the King of Jerusalem forever? This will mean peace in Jerusalem, for He will be married to the city, this land and His bride forever.

Chapter 8

Jerusalem "on That Day"

"This is the word of the LORD concerning Israel. The LORD, who stretches out the heavens, who lays the foundation of the earth, and who forms the spirit of man within him, declares: 'I am going to make Jerusalem a cup that sends all the surrounding peoples reeling. Judah will be besieged as well as Jerusalem. On that day, when all the nations of the earth are gathered against her, I will make Jerusalem an immovable rock for all the nations. All who try to move it will injure themselves. On that day I will strike every horse with panic and its rider with madness,' declares the Lord. 'I will keep a watchful eye over the house of Judah, but I will blind all the horses of the nations. Then the leaders of Judah will say in their hearts, 'The people of Jerusalem are strong, because the LORD Almighty is their God'" (Zechariah 12:1-5).

The Promises of God for Jerusalem

The prophet Zechariah was a man whose own destiny and call was intertwined with the history of Jerusalem. From his vantage point on the Mount of Olives, he witnessed the rebuilding of the temple after the captives had returned from Babylon. He saw how, blinded in the eyes by their limited understanding, the people were discouraged with the building of the second temple. They lost sight of their true vision and lost heart when they compared their effort to Solomon's first temple and found their handiwork lacking. With stirring words, the prophet rallied them to their appointed task, reminding them of God's faithfulness to His people and assuring them that He was with them even in this effort. As he looked down over the city from the very Mount of Olives where Yeshua Himself later wept over Jerusalem, Zechariah also painted a picture of the far distant future. He spoke in deeply moving terms about the destruction of a city he obviously loved. Since we are living in a generation of restoration, many of Zechariah's prophetic declarations can apply to us.

The prophet's very name is a testimony to the faithfulness of God, for his name means, "The Lord remembers." Zechariah exhorts his people to hold to the promises of God and to remember God's faithfulness throughout history. Notice how the prophet begins, **"Return to me," says the Lord of Hosts, "and I will return to you!" (Zechariah 1:2)** These verses remain a timeless reminder to us that God will not forsake us. Zechariah tells those in Jerusalem what they already knew—that God did not stop at their exile and dispersion. Instead, God remembered what He had promised and acted to fulfill these promises.

Zechariah's name is a challenge as well as an encouragement to us as intercessors. One definition of an intercessor is someone who reminds God of His promises to His people. It is a profound testimony to the reality of intercession that God gives us the privilege of reminding Him of what He has promised. In these days of great political and economic uncertainty, it is important to remind God of His promises to us.

The book of Zechariah is also the book in the Bible that makes the most mention of the city of Jerusalem. This is one reason the book is so special to me. Since 1987 I have lived on the Mount of Olives, directly overlooking the Temple Mount. The Garden of Gethsemane is close by. When the Lord called us to establish Jerusalem House of Prayer for All Nations, He directed us, not to the newer Jerusalem as we had anticipated, but to the Mount of Olives, the very place where Yeshua is to return. Our ministry there is to be watchmen, waiting and praying for the coming of the Messiah and encouraging other believers around the world to do the same. In our community, Jewish, Arab and believers from many nations come together to prepare for the coming of the Messiah.

At the end of the age, when the purposes of God have been accomplished, all the nations of the earth will come up against the city of Jerusalem in a final battle. That will be a terrible day. Scripture calls it the great and terrible day of the Lord. It will certainly be a day to know whose side we are on, for the calamities which will strike will be serious.

Sixteen Events "*on That Day*" from the Book of Zechariah

Zechariah 12:3

> "On that day, when all the nations of the earth are gathered against her [Jerusalem], I will make Jerusalem an immovable rock for all nations. All who try to move it will injure themselves."

It will be impossible to change the purposes of God. Those who try to divert the course of events will find that they hurt only themselves. It will be too late to change anything. God's purposes will prevail, no matter what the enemy tries to do! After giving all of humanity ample warning, God allows mankind to be cornered by the inevitable fulfilment of His purposes. As believers dwelling in Israel and among the nations, we need to remember that we are standing on the unmovable rock—Jesus, the King of Jerusalem—for His promises to Jerusalem.

Zechariah 12:4

> "On that day, I will strike every horse with panic and its rider with madness," declares the LORD. "I will keep a watchful eye over Judah, but I will blind all the horses of the nations."

Panic, madness and blindness were curses of God against the Israelites for their disobedience. Now, in the final days of history, God will turn those curses against the enemies of the Jews. The horses, which are necessary to take the warriors to battle, will be blinded. They will not be able to find their way. Although enemies will be gathered around Jerusalem, waiting to destroy it, they will be unable to find their way to their goal. To some extent we can say that the nations are already blinded for they do not understand God's purposes for Israel, and they attempt to superimpose their own plans upon the fate of this nation. However, the Church should not be blinded and should be standing with Jerusalem because God has given His Church eyes to see and ears to hear. God wants the Church to be watching over Jerusalem and the land of Israel.

Zechariah 12:6-7

> "On that day, I will make the leaders of Judah like a firepot in a woodpile, like a flaming torch among sheaves. They will consume right and left all the surrounding people, but Jerusalem will remain intact in her place."

Despite the ravages all around, the Lord will save the dwellings of Judah first so that the honor of the house of David and of Jerusalem's inhabitants will shield those who live in Jerusalem.

Zechariah 12:8

> "On that day, the LORD will shield those who live in Jerusalem, so that the feeblest among them will be like David, and the house of David will be like God, like the Angel of the LORD going before them."

As long as we stand for Jerusalem, we will have shields of protection, no matter where we live in the world. Supernatural strength will be given to those in Jerusalem, so that even the weakest among them will rise up with the strength of David as he went into battle.

The Lord has built a worship shield over Jerusalem: in Jerusalem and from the ends of the earth!

Zechariah 12:9

> "On that day, I will set out to destroy all nations that come up against Jerusalem."

Ultimate destruction will be the fate of those who dare to rise up against Jerusalem. The nations of the world will gather around Jerusalem thinking that they are going to destroy the city, but in reality God will have brought them there to judge them. God will be revealed as the Judge of the nations in Jerusalem so that He can then be revealed as the Prince of Peace for the nations from the city of Jerusalem.

Zechariah 12:11

> "On that day, the weeping in Jerusalem will be great, like the weeping of Hadad Rimmon in the plain of Meggido."

In the verse immediately preceding this statement, Zechariah prophesies that **"They [the Jewish people] will look upon him whom they have pierced. They will mourn for him as one mourns for an only child, and grieve for him as one grieves for a firstborn son."** As the Jewish people realize what they have done to their Messiah, they will be smitten with grief and the sounds of their weeping will be great, as the sounds of mourning for a dead king of Israel. As we approach the final coming of the Lord and as the nations come against Jerusalem, the Jewish people will realize that they have missed their Messiah. When they see that they had to go through all the suffering of the past, including the Holocaust, because they rejected their Messiah, they will weep with broken hearts. In that day, the veil will be pulled away from the eyes of the Jewish people, and they will see their Messiah.

Zechariah 13:1

> "On that day, a fountain will be opened to the house of David and the inhabitants of Jerusalem to cleanse them from sin and impurity."

The house of David is the Jewish people. The inhabitants of Jerusalem include Arabs. God is going to cleanse them from sin, and they will banish their idols. Only the Great King of Jerusalem will be worshiped eternally. Only one Messiah, one God, will be worshiped, and all false gods and religions will be destroyed. The God of Abraham, Isaac and Jacob will be acknowledged as the only true God.

Zechariah 13:2

> "On that day, I will banish the names of the idols from the land, and they will be remembered no more," declares the LORD Almighty. "I will remove both the prophets and the spirit of impurity from the land."

Here, the Lord promises that all forms of idolatry, including humanism, icons, Freemasonry, Kabbalah, Islam and anything else that has set itself up against the knowledge of God will be destroyed.

Zechariah 13:4

"On that day, every prophet will be ashamed of his prophetic vision. He will not put on a prophet's garment of hair in order to deceive. He will say, 'I am not a prophet. I am a farmer, the land has been my livelihood since my youth.'"

The Bible says we know in part and we prophesy in part. God wants us to speak forth a pure prophetic word in these days because a day is coming soon when every prophet will be ashamed of himself. The Bible tells us that in the former days, God spoke through the prophets. In the latter days, He is going to speak to us through His Son. We can only be a pure prophetic voice to the degree that we are in one accord with the Son, because He is the true Prophet, Priest and King today. He wants us to be His voices to speak forth His prophetic word.

Zechariah 14:4

"On that day, his feet will stand on the Mount of Olives, east of Jerusalem, and the Mount of Olives will be split in two from east to west, forming a great valley, with half of the mountain moving north and half moving south."

Yeshua is coming back to the Mount of Olives. His arrival is not going to be quiet and unpretentious. Trumpets will announce His arrival and the earth will split in two as He puts His feet upon the ground. In verse 2 of this chapter, the prophet describes the destruction of Jerusalem, telling us that **"the city will be captured and the women raped. Half of the city will go into exile but the rest of the people will not be taken from the city."** Many Joshuas and Calebs are going to be left standing at the return of the Messiah and will be there to see Him come. Some will flee; some will be driven out but half will remain. Imagine being one of those staying until the end and to be able to witness the sight of Yeshua descending upon the Mount of Olives. Imagine the incredible sight and the awesome noise of the earth splitting and moving north and south and our Lord and King in His City forever.

Zechariah 14:6-7

> "On that day, there will be no light, no cold or frost. It will be a unique day, without daytime or nighttime—a day known to the LORD. When evening comes, there will be light."

Zechariah 14:8

> "On that day, living water will flow out from Jerusalem, half to the eastern sea and half to the western sea, in summer and in winter."

The Dead Sea, which is now an unmoving body of water, will be brought to life once again. It will be full of fish and plants, and will be much better than the Sea of Galilee since it is about 50 times larger. It will be a wonderful sea to swim in. Living waters will flow from Jerusalem to the Mediterranean sea as well.

Zechariah 14:9

> "On that day there will be one LORD, and his name the only name."

All false Gods and idols will be banished. Only His name will be exalted.

Zechariah 14:13

> "On that day men will be stricken by the LORD with great panic. Each man will seize the hand of another, and they will attack each other."

Prior to this, the Prophet describes the fate of the enemies of Israel. He tells us that **"their flesh will rot while they are still standing on their feet, and their tongues will rot in their mouths and their eyes will rot in their sockets" (v.12).** As they witness their own destruction and realized that their plans for Jerusalem have backfired against them, they will turn on those they are with. There will be no more unity among the attackers, but they will turn on one another in their terror.

Zechariah 14:20

> **"On that day, HOLY TO THE LORD will be inscribed on the bells of horses and the cooking pots in the LORD's house will be like sacred bowls in front of the altar."**

Even the most basic utensils of life become holy when brought before the presence of God. There will be nothing too small, too insignificant, too ordinary that it will not be made holy before God.

Zechariah 14:21

> **"On that day there will no longer be a Canaanite in the house of the LORD Almighty."**

This will be the ultimate "Jerusalem Day" for this will truly mark the celebration of the King of Jerusalem as He comes into His city. This time will represent the fulfillment of God's purposes and all things on this earth will be brought under His rule and dominion. There will no longer be any need to take the Messiah's supper, as important as that is for believers in Yeshua, for Scripture tells us that we must take the Lord's Supper until He returns. When He returns, we will not need to be reminded of His death and His resurrection any longer, since we will see Him with the nailprints in His hands and feet, risen and victorious in our midst. When He comes back to put His feet on the Mount of Olives, the finished work of the cross, the significance of communion and His second coming will all converge into one glorious moment of total victory.

The final rule of Yeshua the Messiah is marked by the above 16 separate sets of circumstances and events. Abraham was looking forward to the day of the Lord. He was looking to more than the crucifixion that was represented by the sacrifices of Melchizedek. He was also looking towards the very end, to the time when Yeshua would put His feet on the Mount of Olives. He was ultimately looking forward to the fulfillment of what the apostle John writes,

> "And he carried me away in the Spirit to a mountain great and high, and showed me the Holy City, Jerusalem, coming down out of heaven from God. It shone with the glory of God, and its brilliance was like that of a very precious jewel, like a jasper, clear as crystal" (Revelation 21:10).

The scripture continues to describe that the wall of the city had 12 foundations and on them were the names of the 12 apostles of the Lamb.

Abraham was looking forward to this complete revelation of the Lord Yeshua, but many revelations had to come to pass and must still be fulfilled, before we are able to see the fullness that Abraham was looking for in the book of Genesis. Because we have the last chapter of the story, we know how it will end, that the all the promises for Jerusalem will come to pass.

In Revelation 21:22, John continues to describe the new Jerusalem and tells us that "I did not see a temple in the city, because the LORD God Almighty and the Lamb are its temple." Yeshua will return once more to rule and reign as King over Jerusalem. He has been King over this city since the time of Melchizedek. Throughout the whole of the Old Testament, He has been King over Jerusalem, and He died as King of Jerusalem. Most of the inhabitants of that city did not recognize Him, although He died as King of the Jews in Jerusalem, as was written on the top of the cross. He trampled over all the power of the enemy and rendered the enemy powerless through the cross. He was resurrected as the King of Jerusalem and is coming back to put His feet on the Mount of Olives. He will bring full spiritual deliverance as well as the spiritual liberation of Jerusalem. As the new Jerusalem comes down from heaven, there will be no need for a physical temple of stone and rock because the Lamb is the temple and we are the stones. What remains the most significant is not that Jerusalem is a wonderful city, but that the Great King has chosen to manifest Himself through Jerusalem. It is only through the presence of her King that Jerusalem acquires her eternal value.

We must covenant to stand with the Lord on behalf of His city, Jerusalem, because He has promised to reveal Himself in the events and actions that surround this city. If we want to stand with Him, if we want to agree with His purposes and participate in His plans, then we must stand with the Lord for Jerusalem. He is going to reveal Himself to the Muslims. He is going to reveal Himself to the Jews as they are gathered from the nations and He is going to reveal Himself in the Church, His Body, as it becomes unified under one King. The law will go forth from Zion and the Word of the Lord from Jerusalem. Many evangelists will go forth with the Word of God from Jerusalem. The nations will be judged at Jerusalem. Yeshua is coming back to reign over the earth forever as the new Jerusalem comes down from heaven.

Pray for these 16 prophetic promises to be fulfilled and settled on earth and in Jerusalem as they have been settled in heaven. As you are praying for these things to come to fullness, you are praying for the peace of Jerusalem. As you stand with the Lord as a faithful watchman over Jerusalem, we pray the Lord will prosper you.

Chapter 9

I Myself Will Be a Wall of Fire Around Jerusalem and Her Glory Within

From the Ends of the Earth to Jerusalem

"Jerusalem will be a city without walls because of the great number of men and livestock in it. And I myself will be a wall of fire around it," declares the Lord, "and I will be its glory within" (Zechariah 2:4-5).

We truly live in the last days that the prophet Zechariah refers to in chapter 2. While it is clear that these things are beginning to happen and more will happen soon, there is much we can do to prepare the way.

In the first century, the Jewish believers took the Gospel from Jerusalem to Judea, Samaria and to the ends of the then known earth. After the day of Pentecost, Peter went to Rome; John Mark to Egypt and Africa; John to Europe and Turkey; Thomas to India; Paul to Asia and Europe. Christianity has since grown to be the religion with the most adherents (approximately two billion) in the world.

In 1988, Youth With A Mission took torches from the Mount of Olives in Jerusalem where the Great Commission was given, to the ends of the earth, believing God for the fulfillment of the Great Commission by the end of the year 2000.

In February 2000, I was ministering in Australia at a conference where the Olympic torches for the 2000 Olympic Games later that year were about to be lit. The Lord woke me up at 3 am and began to speak to me about it being time to bring the torches back to Jerusalem from the ends of the earth. I did not know what this meant until I turned to Judges 6 and realized that 300 torches were lit by Gideon and his army, while at the same time they blew 300 *shofars*. In 1998, at All Nations Convocation Jerusalem, we blew 300 *shofars*; and in 2000, the Lord was showing us to also light 300 torches! The Lord showed that He had built a wall of revival fire around Jerusalem from the ends of the earth, and it was time for the wall of fire to move through the nations back to Jerusalem. We were to bring torches from the ends of the earth through the nations back to Jerusalem, believing God for all nations to be lit prophetically. This is already happening.

The Latin American revival has touched North America and Europe, as the revival fire is spreading, coming closer to Jerusalem. The Spanish-speaking nations are planning to plant 1,000 churches in Spain. El Salvador and Costa Rica are the only two nations in the world to have their embassies in Jerusalem, recognizing Jerusalem as the City of the Great King. The revival in Brazil is now impacting Portugal.

Isaiah 19:22-23 says there will be a big highway (fire) from Africa (Egypt) to Israel. This is beginning to happen in Nigeria, Uganda, Tanzania, South Africa and Kenya. I joined with almost five million believers in Nigeria for an all-night prayer meeting for 11 hours. They prayed for Israel and blew a shofar over North Africa to Jerusalem. Since then God has given Nigeria a born-again president and the revival is increasing. Many breakthroughs are happening in Nigeria, North Africa and Israel.

God is also moving in a powerful way in India. Many are coming to the Lord in southern India where thousands have died as martyrs including the apostle Thomas. In Nepal there were virtually no believers 30 years ago. Today almost one million profess faith in Jesus in the place where Buddhism and Hinduism were born. The highest place in the world is being taken for Jesus!

Today in China almost 100 million people profess faith in Jesus. China probably has one of the two largest populations of born-again believers in the world, especially in the south of the country.

The circle of fire continues through Asia to Indonesia, where great revival is experienced now. Some say there are 50 million believers in this nation. Their boldness in evangelism, prevailing prayer and worship in the midst of persecution are a great testimony to the whole world. One pastor just finished a church building for 20,000 believers. There are churches of over 100,000 people in this nation.

God is also moving through the Philippines. I spoke there at a church of one million believers and many more are coming to know Jesus. Many are also planning to bring the fire back to Jerusalem.

Korea continues to have a big impact in carrying the fire through Central Asia to Jerusalem. Russia, Ukraine and other nations of the former Soviet Union are experiencing great revival. Over one million Jews have come home to Israel from these northern nations in the last 12 years, bringing thousands of Russian Jewish believers to Israel. They are the leading force in Israel today.

We know that Brownsville, Pensacola, has had a big impact in bringing the fire to Europe and Israel. So we can see that the circle of fire is coming from the ends of the earth through the nations to Jerusalem.

On October 12, 2000, in Tel Aviv, we passed 300 torches from all nations to the Jewish and Arab believers in Israel, believing God for Jerusalem and Israel's salvation. God promised that the salvation of Israel and Jerusalem would be like a blazing torch (Isa. 62:1). In Genesis 13, Abraham saw God as a blazing torch passing between the pieces of the animal sacrifice, signifying the division between Ishmael (Gentile) and Isaac (Jew).

Today, we live in days of restoration and reconciliation. God promised to make Egypt, Israel and Assyria a blessing in the midst of the earth. The sons of Ishmael and Isaac will be reunited and will worship God together. Zechariah 12 says God will make the leaders of Judah as a firepot in a woodpile and a flaming torch among sheaves.

From Heaven to Jerusalem

The title of this chapter is taken from Zechariah 2:5 in which the Lord promises to be a wall of fire around Jerusalem and her glory within. The

Lord says, **"The earth will be filled with the knowledge of the glory of the LORD as the waters cover the sea"** (Habakkuk 2:14). He is releasing His fire from heaven through His people from revivals at the ends of the earth, moving in restoration from the nations back to Jerusalem.

The ultimate focal point of the manifestation of His fire and glory will be released from heaven to Jerusalem. The Lord Himself will become a wall of fire around Jerusalem and her glory within. Israel is the fire and Jerusalem is the furnace (Isa. 31:9). For those living in Jerusalem in the last days, life will increasingly be like Shadrach, Meshach and Abednego's experience in the fiery furnace. God said:

> **"See, I will send my messenger, who will prepare the way before me. Then suddenly the Lord you are seeking will come to this temple; the messenger of the covenant, whom you desire will come," says the LORD Almighty.**
>
> **But who can endure the day of his coming? Who can stand when he appears? For he will be like a refiner's fire or a launderer's soap. He will sit as a refiner and purifier of silver; he will purify the Levites and refine them like gold and silver. Then the LORD will have men who will bring offerings in righteousness, and the offerings of Judah and Jerusalem will be acceptable to the LORD, as in days gone by, as in former years"** (Malachi 3:2-4).

Among the last verses of the *Tanach* (Old Testament), God says,

> **"'Surely the day is coming; it will burn like a furnace. All the arrogant and every evildoer will be stubble, and that day that is coming will set them on fire,' says the LORD Almighty. ... 'But for you who revere my name, the sun of righteousness [the King of Jerusalem] will rise with healing in its wings"** (Malachi 4:1-2).

In verse 5, God promises to send the prophet Elijah, who will turn the hearts of the fathers to their children, and hearts of the children to their fathers. In 1 Kings 18:24, Elijah said that the God who answers by fire, He is God. We know that Elijah was the prophet who called fire from heaven and then slew hundreds of Baal prophets. If he is to turn the hearts of the fathers and the children to each other, it will be because the fire of God will burn away the filth that separates people from Him.

May the God who answers by fire turn the Jews to the Arabs and the Arabs to the Jews as His consuming fire purifies them. May the hearts of the fathers also be turned to the children and the children to the fathers.

24-Hour Worship and Intercession

Another way we can stand in the gap for the people in Israel and the Middle East, is through 24-hour worship and intercession. The Lord is already birthing the 24-hour Watch of the Lord on the 12 Gates of Jerusalem, even as it is in heaven.

We live in the days of the restoration of David's tabernacle and Solomon's temple. It is time to build according to the pattern in heaven where they are encircling the throne in worship. The Jewish people have always worshiped facing Jerusalem from wherever they are in the world. It is time, not only for the gates of Jerusalem to open up, preparing the way for the King of Glory to come in, but it is also time for the gates of the nations to open up for the people from the nations to welcome the King as they face Jerusalem. Believers in the nations need to join in 24-hour worship and intercession as part of the wall of fire around and the shield of worship covering Jerusalem from the ends of the earth. As they do this, they will be building altars and pillars of 24-hour worship from the 12 Gateway regions of the world towards the 12 Gates of Jerusalem. This will help prepare the way for the people of Jerusalem and the whole earth to be filled with the knowledge of the glory of the Lord as the waters cover the sea. The King of Glory will be fully revealed and will come to take up His throne in His city forever.

There will be 12 Gates on the new Jerusalem when it comes out of heaven. Today, God is establishing 24-hour worship and intercession on the 12 Gates as a prophetic first-fruit, preparing the way for when all things in heaven and on earth will become one in the Messiah. Then He will take up His throne as the place of the soles of His feet forever on the Temple Mount.

There are two maps towards the back of this book explaining the World Wide Watch strategy of surrounding Jerusalem with worship from the ends of the earth. It also explains the time that you can worship on the gates of Jerusalem, based on Israel time, to cover the city with a shield of worship. We need you to stand with us worshiping and interceding as the World Wide Watch from your gateway to the nations. Contact us for more details.

We need to stand together as watchmen from the nations, the Middle East and Israel, believing God to answer by fire. He is the God who answers by fire, and will bring Jerusalem's salvation by releasing the fullness of His fire from heaven to fully burn up the idols and prophets of Baal as well as the Babylonian influences that try to hinder His purposes. We need to trust the Lord that the fullness of revival fire will come to Jerusalem, the furnace.

The book of Hebrews talks about believers coming to Mount Zion; to the heavenly Jerusalem; to the city of the living God, to thousands upon thousands of angels in joyful assembly; and to the Church of the firstborn whose names are written in heaven (Heb. 12). When the people of the earthly Jerusalem receive the heavenly Jerusalem, they will experience these things in fullness as all things in heaven and earth are joined in fullness in Yeshua when He takes up the throne of David on the Temple Mount. Hebrews 12 continues to warn us: **"See to it that you do not refuse him who speaks"** in the midst of God shaking everything. God says He will shake everything that can be shaken, but He has also promised a **"kingdom that cannot be shaken,"** because **"our God is a consuming fire."**

In Revelation 1:14-16, when Yeshua, the Messiah, is revealed to John, His eyes are like blazing fire and His face like the sun shining in all of its brilliance. His feet are like bronze, glowing in a furnace. In Revelation 4, when John is caught up before the throne in heaven, there came from the throne flashes of lightning, rumblings and peals of thunders. Before the throne are seven lamps, blazing with fire. These are the seven spirits of God. In the center of the throne are the four living creatures. Day and night they never stop saying: **"Holy, holy, holy is the Lord God Almighty, who was, and is and is to come."**

As we move from one millennium to another, God wants the fire that never stops burning in the lamp of heaven 24 hours a day to be lit continually and never stop burning in the 24-hour Watches He is birthing in all the nations and in Jerusalem.

> The LORD said to Moses: "Give Aaron and his sons this command: 'These are the regulations for the burnt offering: The burnt offering is to remain on the altar hearth throughout the night, till morning, and the fire must be kept burning on the altar. ... The fire on the altar must be kept burning; it must not go out. Every morning the priest is to add firewood and arrange the burnt offering on the fire and burn the fat of the fellowship offerings on it. The fire must be kept burning on the altar continuously; it must not go out'" (Leviticus 6:8-9,12-13).

Even as the fire never stops burning on the altar and in the lamp in heaven, God's heart and purpose is that the same thing will be done with the lamps and altars of the watches that He is birthing throughout the nations that are turning back towards Jerusalem. When God made a covenant with Abraham, the old patriarch had to cut the sacrifices in half. A smoking firepot and blazing torch appeared and passed between the pieces (Gen. 15: 17). In the chapter following this event, Ishmael and Isaac are born.

Praying for the Peace of Jerusalem Means Praying for Her People

As we pray for the peace of Jerusalem, we need to pray that the two pieces which are the two peoples, the Arabs and Jews that live in this land that God promised to Abraham, will be reconciled; that a blazing firepot and a blazing torch will appear to them, burning away the dross that separates them and that they would be purified through the refiner's fire. Pray that they will prepare to be the blessing in the midst of the earth that God has destined them to become.

Zechariah 12 says that Jerusalem and Judah will become like a firepot in a woodpile, like a flaming torch among sheaves. Isaiah 62:1 says that

Jerusalem's salvation will be as a blazing torch. As we continue to pray for the peace of Jerusalem, we need to pray that all of us, including the Jewish and Arab believers in Egypt, Israel and Assyria, will receive the torch from heaven and that we will see many 24-hour Watches birthed, not only in the nations but also in all Arab nations and Israel. Pray also that the fires will never go out, but that they will be kept burning continuously day and night. This will prepare the way for the fullness of Israel's salvation to be released like a blazing torch and the Lord Himself will become a wall of fire around Jerusalem and her glory within when He comes to His temple in Jerusalem in fullness. The fires burning on the altars in heaven and throughout the earth will then be joined into one flame in Jerusalem for eternity.

Pray that the people in the region of Egypt, Israel and Assyria will receive salvation and a fresh outpouring of the Holy Spirit and fire.

When we pray for the peace of Jerusalem, our prayers have primarily to do not with politics, but with people. Praying for the peace of Jerusalem involves praying for the unity of Jews and Arabs and the outpouring of the Holy Spirit and fire on them. Pray also for Jewish and Arab pastors and believers inside the walls of the Old City, as well as in the whole of the modern city of Jerusalem. It also involves praying for the people in the whole land of Israel, as Jerusalem will be the capital of all of this land.

Furthermore, God has promised His people the land from the Nile to the Euphrates, so ultimately Jerusalem represents/is the capital of this whole area.

> "A smoking firepot with a blazing torch appeared and passed between the pieces. On that day the LORD made a covenant with Abraham and said, 'To your descendants I give this land, from the river of Egypt to the great river, the Euphrates'" (Genesis 15:19).

We need to pray that God will hasten the day when He will make the people in this region of Egypt, Israel and Assyria a blessing in the midst of the earth.

We will see tremendous shakings take place in these last days, in Jerusalem, Israel and the Arab Middle East. The Lord will begin to manifest Himself as a "wall of fire around Jerusalem" and as "her glory within." I encourage you to read Isaiah chapters 11 through 19 to better understand what God will do in the last days in the Middle East. However, these shakings will be redemptive, as seen in the culmination of events in Isaiah 19:23-25.

It also appears that before the Gog–Magog war, there will be another war that will bring great shakings and may bring about the collapse of many of the forces of darkness that are opposing Israel and the Arab Middle East today. Ezekiel 38 implies that this will have happened before the Gog–Magog war.

> "After many days you [Gog and Magog] will be called to arms. In future years you will invade a land that has recovered from war, whose peoples were gathered from many nations to the mountains of Israel which have long been desolate. They have been brought out of many nations and now all of them live in safety ... You will say, I will invade a land of unwalled villages. I will attack a peaceful, unsuspecting people. All of them living without walls and without gates and bars."

What is spoken of in this passage is surely not the case in the Middle East today. From this scripture and Isaiah 19:23-25 it appears that Egypt, Israel and Assyria, being a blessing in the midst of the earth, could come into place at least partially before the coming of the Lord and before the Gog–Magog war. It says that the invaders will come to a **"peaceful, unsuspecting people."** This peaceful state could refer to a land in which the highway of Isaiah 19:23-25 runs through, and the people are a blessing in the midst of the earth.

The title of Dr. Peter Wagner's book, *Prayer Shield*, was taken from Zechariah 12, but it was spiritualized for believers and the Church. However, the literal context of this verse has to do with the Lord shielding those who live in Jerusalem in the last days.

Through your prayers, help prepare the way for the Kingdom of God to come on earth as it is in heaven, that the gates of the city would be opened and the doors lifted up, that the King of Glory will come into the hearts of His people in Jerusalem. Pray that His resting place may be prepared for the dove, the Holy Spirit, to fill Jerusalem with His glory so the fullness of His cloud of glory would be manifested.

Pray, as God is shaking everything that can be shaken in this region in these years, that all Babylonian influence of false gods, false religions, covenants of death, false messiahs and every refuge of lies will be broken off from the people. Pray that they will be born from above and arise together to kiss the Son of righteousness and justice, the King and Salvation of Jerusalem, who has deliverance, healing and salvation in His wings.

Pray for the spiritual liberation of the people of Jerusalem, that the yokes and chains will be broken off from their necks, spirits and bodies. May they, in the coming day of battle, put on the Lord Jesus as a shield of faith and arise in worship, proclamation and prayer. May the Lord Himself be a shield over Jerusalem as they arise in faith and the feeblest one among them become like King David and that the house of David may become like God. May the Lord open a fountain over the house of David and all the inhabitants of Jerusalem (Zech. 12).

Pray for the fullness of the people in Jerusalem (Jews, Arabs, internationals) to be born again and for the fullness of Christ, the Messiah, to be formed in them. He alone is the mystery hidden from all ages, the Messiah in us the hope of glory (Col. 1:27). Ephesians 5 tells us that a man being married to his wife and becoming one flesh is a profound mystery as is Christ being married to the Church. I hope this book gives you some revelation and understanding of this mystery of King Yeshua being married to Jerusalem. In the end this profound mystery will only be fully revealed with Messiah's coming to bring all things in heaven and earth into one, in Him. Until that time, keep waiting, worshiping, working and praying for Jerusalem's peace to shine as a blazing torch! Pray for His glory to completely fill His temple of living stones in Jerusalem, that He will be a wall of fire around Jerusalem and her glory within.

Ways You Can Pray for the People and Peace of Jerusalem Today:

1. Pray for the unity of all elders sitting at the 12 Gates of Jerusalem—Jewish, Arab and international. Pray for the fullness of the ascension gift ministries of apostles, prophets, pastors, teachers and evangelists, to be given from heaven and received in Jerusalem on earth (Eph. 4:7-13).

2. Pray for a corporate gift of unity, repentance, reconciliation, restoration and revival.

3. Pray that God will pour out a spirit of prayer and supplication, that they will mourn for the One whom they have pierced.

4. Pray that the Lord will raise up more indigenous labourers for the harvest, for the harvest is ripe, but the laborers are few.

5. Pray that none among them will lack anything.

6. Pray that the Lord will be a shield over the people of Jerusalem.

7. Pray that the feeblest one among them will be like King David and that the house of David will be like God.

8. Pray that Jerusalem's salvation will become like a blazing torch.

9. Pray that the people will open up the gates and doors of their hearts that the King of Glory may come into their hearts and the city in a fuller sense.

10. Pray that the Lord will bring to fullness the 24-hour worship on the gates of Jerusalem. Pray that the apostolic–elder gatekeepers and worshiping, interceding gatekeepers in Jerusalem and in His whole body may be greatly unified and strengthened.

11. Pray that God will use the annual All Jerusalem, All Israel, All Middle East and All Nations Convocations Jerusalem to help facilitate His Kingdom coming to Jerusalem and the nations even as it is in heaven.

12. Pray for the coming of the Lord, that the believers in Jerusalem, the bride, will make herself ready to be married to the King of Jerusalem for eternity.

Pray for the people of Jerusalem on an ongoing basis. If you contact or visit us, we can put you in contact with the elders and worshiping gate-keepers on the 12 Gates of Jerusalem and different congregations within the city to help you have personal contact with the people of Jerusalem in a fuller way. Then you will be able to pray more effectively for her peace.

Praying for the peace of Jerusalem is all about Messiah and how He is revealing Himself to His people—Jews and Arabs in the Middle East and believers from all nations—until her salvation shines like a blazing torch. We are calling God's watchmen on the walls from all nations to join with us in the gap on the gates, in the trenches and on the walls of Jerusalem. Your participation with us is vital to win the battle for Jerusalem in these last days.

Continue praying with us for Messiah to progressively reveal Himself to His people and for the ten stones to be completely removed. Help to prepare the way for the King of Jerusalem to be fully revealed to Jews and Arabs. This will culminate in Messiah as a blazing torch taking up the throne of David in Jerusalem, the place of the soles of His feet forever. Let the fire fall. Let the torch be released from heaven and also the torches of worship and intercession from the ends of the earth preparing the way for the Lord Himself to be a wall of fire around Jerusalem and her glory within.

The seven maps and pictures in Appendix 1 may help you to better understand God's progressive purposes from the Fall of man—Jerusalem in the Garden of Eden-Paradise—to the full restoration of the new Jerusalem coming down from heaven as a beautifully dressed bride for her husband.

Jerusalem's History and Future in Maps and Pictures

You have not finished reading this book until you have studied the seven maps and pictures that describe seven different significant times in the development of Jerusalem from the Garden of Eden to the new Jerusalem.

These maps and pictures show God's original, redemptive, progressive and ultimate purposes in history in regard to Jerusalem. I hope these pictures will help you to better understand God's destiny for Jerusalem and bring fuller clarity and vision to the message of this book.

1. Where Was the Garden of Eden?
Genesis 2:8-14

"When the sun had set and darkness had fallen, a smoking firepot with a blazing torch (see this book's cover) appeared and passed between the pieces. On that day the Lord made a covenant with Abram and said, 'To your descendants I give this land, from the river of Egypt to the great river, the Euphrates'" (Genesis 15:17-18).

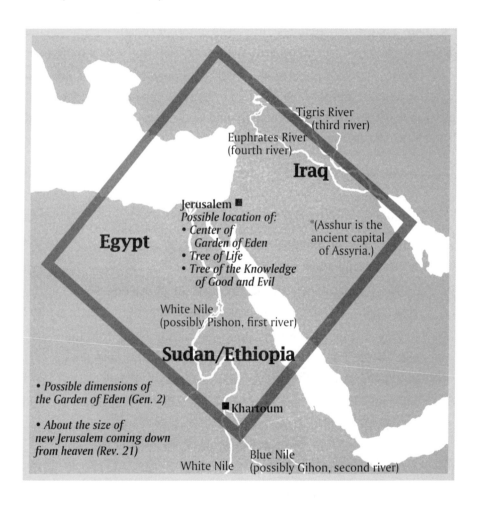

God promised that again Egypt, Israel and Assyria will become a blessing in the midst of the earth (Isa. 19:23-25). He will also eventually bring the new Jerusalem down from heaven (Rev. 21). The city will be 12,000 stadia (1,400 miles) high, long and wide—a distance that covers the Middle East from the Nile to the Euphrates River.

> "Now the Lord God had planted a garden in the east, in Eden; and there he put the man he had formed. And the Lord God made all kinds of trees grow out of the ground—trees that were pleasing to the eye and good for food. In the middle of the garden were the tree of life and the tree of the knowledge of good and evil.
>
> "A river watering the garden flowed from Eden; from there it was separated into four headwaters. The name of the first is the Pishon; it winds through the entire land of Havilah, where there is gold. (The gold of that land is good; aromatic resin and onyx are also there.) The name of the second river is the Gihon; it winds through the entire land of Cush. The name of the third river is the Tigris; it runs along the east side of Asshur. And the fourth river is the Euphrates" (Genesis 2:8-14).

188 PRAY FOR THE PEACE OF JERUSALEM

2. Was Abraham's Journey a Prayer Walk To Rebuild First-Fruits Foundations of the Garden of Eden?

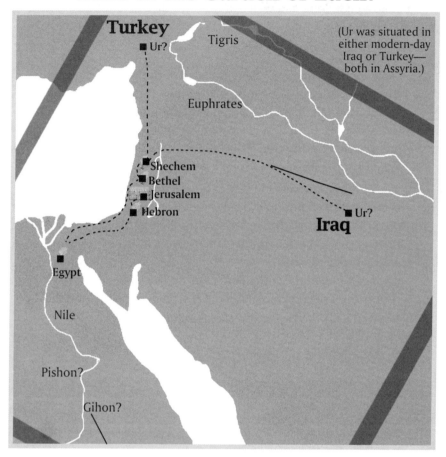

Abraham walked across the Promised Land from Ur in Assyria, through Israel to Egypt and built altars at Shechem and Bethel on his way. He then traveled to Egypt during a famine but returned to build altars at Hebron and Jerusalem (where God stopped him short of sacrificing Isaac (in the center of the garden). Abraham was the father of us all; Jews, Arabs and people from all nations are all children of Abraham by faith. Jesus said Abraham saw His day and was glad (he saw the crucifixion of Jesus). He also saw the new Jerusalem coming down out of heaven, with foundations and whose builder and maker was God (Heb. 11:8-10).

3. David—Solomon's Kingdom

"When Solomon finished praying, fire came down from heaven and consumed the burnt offering and the sacrifices, and the glory of the Lord filled the temple. The priests could not enter the temple of the LORD because the glory of the LORD filled it" (2 Chronicles 7:1-2).

"He [Solomon] ruled over all the kings from the River [Euphrates] to the land of the Philistines, as far as the border of Egypt (2 Chronicles 9:26).

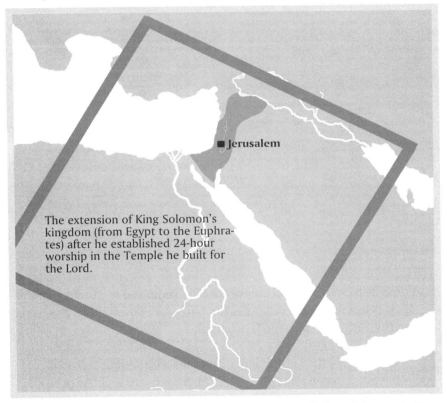

The extension of King Solomon's kingdom (from Egypt to the Euphrates) after he established 24-hour worship in the Temple he built for the Lord.

It is interesting that God expanded the borders of King Solomon's kingdom to the great river Euphrates after he restored 24-hour worship in the temple! When we are possessed by heaven 24 hours a day, God will give to the Jews and Arabs their earthly possession together and all of us our inheritance in Him.

4. A Cross in the Midst of the Garden

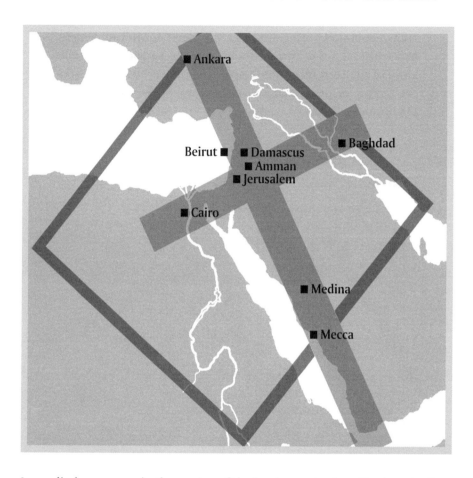

Jesus died on a cross in the center of the land promised to Abraham in Genesis 15. It is interesting to note that the nine main cities in this land today form a cross, with its center in Jerusalem.

> "On that day the Lord made a covenant with Abram and said, 'To your descendants I give this land, from the river of Egypt to the great river, the Euphrates'" (Genesis 15:18).

> "And having disarmed the powers and authorities, he [Jesus] made a public spectacle of them, triumphing over them by the cross" (Colossians 2:15).

Great salvation and reconciliation will be restored as this region of Egypt, Israel and Assyria becomes a blessing in the midst of the earth. I have visited these cities with others to pray for the peace of Jerusalem over a span of ten years, prayer walking from Egypt's border (Nile) through Israel to Assyria (Euphrates).

5a. The First-Fruits of the Restoration of Jerusalem: Egypt, Israel and Assyria Being a Blessing in the Midst of the Earth

"Then I looked up—and there before me was a man with a measuring line in his hand! I asked, 'Where are you going?' He answered me, 'To measure Jerusalem, to find out how wide and how long it is.' Then the angel who was speaking to me left,

WORSHIPPING GOD TOGETHER

Isaiah 19:23-25

and another angel came to meet him and said to him: 'Run, tell that young man, "Jerusalem will be a city without walls because of the great number of men and livestock in it. And I myself will be a wall of fire around it," declares the Lord, "and I will be its glory within"'" (Zechariah 2:1-5).

"After many days you [Gog and Magog] will be called to arms. In future years you will invade a land that has recovered from war, whose people were gathered from many nations to the mountains of Israel, which had long been desolate. .... You will say, 'I will invade a land of unwalled villages; I will attack a peaceful and unsuspecting people—all of them living without walls and without gates and bars'" (Ezekiel 38:8,11).

This seems to say that there will be a war whose results will bring peace to the Middle East before the Gog–Magog war.

"In that day there will be a highway from Egypt to Assyria. The Assyrians will go to Egypt and the Egyptians to Assyria. The Egyptians and Assyrians will worship together. In that day Israel will be the third, along with Egypt and Assyria, a blessing on the earth" (Isaiah 19:23-24).

5b. Prayer Walking the Land Promised to Abraham—from the Nile to the Euphrates—for Jerusalem's Restoration and Jews and Arabs As One New Man

In 1991, we prayer walked in the steps of Abraham, reminding God of His promises to restore this region as a blessing in the midst of the earth. We built altars in 12 places, prayed and worshiped. In 1995 we also prayer walked from Cairo (Egypt), to Israel, Baghdad (Iraq) and Ur (Assyria), believing God for full restoration of Egypt, Israel and Assyria.

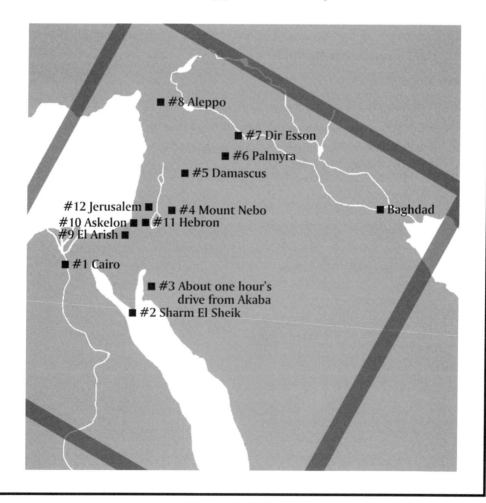

As leaders in the Middle East, we have met together ten times for four days at difficult times during the 1990s for All Middle East Convocations. We now need to pray and work for God to move from first-fruits to fullness. This will climax in the coming of the Lord.

We have seen believers from all Arab nations and Israel worshiping God together. Pray for excellent worship teams from Israel and the Arab Middle East—Jews and Arabs—who will lead millions into worship of God for increasing salvation to come as a blessing in the midst of the earth.

6. Millennial Reign of Messiah
Revelation 5:5

"Do not weep. See the Lion of the tribe of Judah, the root of David has triumphed" (Revelation 5:5).

"Then the man brought me to the gate facing east, and I saw the glory of the God of Israel coming from the east. His voice was like the roar of rushing waters, and the land was radiant with his glory. The vision I saw was like the vision I had seen when he came to destroy the city and like the visions I had seen by the Kebar River, and I fell facedown. The glory of the Lord entered the temple through the gate facing east. Then the Spirit lifted me up and brought me into the inner court, and the glory of the Lord filled the temple. While the man was standing beside me, I heard someone speaking to me from inside the temple. He said: Son of man, this is the place of my throne and the place for the soles of my feet. This is where I will live among the Israelites forever. The house of Israel will never again defile my holy name—neither they nor their kings—by their prostitution and the lifeless idols of their kings at their high places" (Ezekiel 43:1-7).

"And I saw an angel coming down out of heaven, having the key to the Abyss and holding in his hand a great chain. He seized the dragon, that ancient serpent, who is the devil, or Satan, and bound him for a thousand years. He threw him into the Abyss, and locked and sealed it over him, to keep him from deceiving the nations anymore until the thousand years were ended. After that, he must be set free for a short time" (Revelation 20:1-4).

"For to us a child is born, to us a son is given, and the government will be on his shoulders. And he will be called Wonderful Counselor, Mighty God, Everlasting Father, Prince of Peace. Of the increase of his government and peace there will be no end. He will reign on David's throne and over his kingdom, establishing and upholding it with justice and righteousness from that time on and forever. The zeal of the LORD Almighty will accomplish this" (Isaiah 9:6-7).

Some people believe that there is a literal 1000-year reign on earth of Messiah before the new Jerusalem comes down from heaven as this implies. Others believe at His coming we go straight into the new heaven and the new earth.

Jerusalem of Gold

By Naomi Shemer

1. As clear as wine, the wind is flying
Among the dreamy pines
As evening light is slowly dying
And a lonely bell still chimes,
So many songs, so many stories
The stony hills recall….
Around her heart my city carries
A lonely ancient wall.

Yerushalaim all of gold
Yerushalaim, bronze and light
Within my heart I shall treasure
Your song and sight.

2. Alas, the dry wells and fountains,
Forgotten market-day
The sound of horn from Temple's mountain
No longer calls to pray,
The rocky caves at night are haunted
By sounds of long ago
When we were going to the Jordan
By way of Jericho.

3. But when I come to count your praises
And sing Hallel to you
With pretty rhymes I dare not crown you
As other poets do,
Upon my lips
Is always burning
Your name, so dear, so old;
If I forget Yerushalaim
Of bronze and light and gold….

4. Back to the wells and to the fountains
Within the ancient walls
The sound of horn from Temple's mountain
Again so loudly calls,
From rocky caves, this very morning
A thousand suns will glow
As we shall go down to the Jordan
By way of Jericho

The Holy City

Text: FE Weatherly 1892
Music: Stephen Adams 1892

1. Last night I lay asleeping,
There came a dream so fair;
I stood in old Jerusalem
Beside the temple there.
I heard the children singing,
And ever as they sang,
Me thought the voice of angels
From heav'n in answer rang;
Me thought the voice of angels
From heav'n in answer rang.

Jerusalem! Jerusalem!
Lift up your gates and sing,
Hosanna in the highest
Hosanna to your King!

2. And then me thought my dream
was chang'd, The streets no longer rang,
Hush'd were the glad hosannas
The little children sang.
The sun grew dark with mystery,
The morn was cold and chill,
As the shadow of a cross arose
Upon a lonely hill;
As the shadow of a cross arose
Upon a lonely hill.

3. And once again the scene was chang'd,
New earth there seemed to be;
I saw the Holy City
Beside the tideless sea;
The light of God was on its streets,
The gates were open wide,
And all who would might enter,
And no one was denied.
No need of moon or stars by night,
Or sun to shine by day;
It was the new Jerusalem
That would not pass away,
It was the new Jerusalem
That would not pass away.

7. The Holy City, the New Jerusalem, Coming Down Out of Heaven from God, Prepared As a Bride, Beautifully Dressed for Her Husband.

Here we see the final state of Jerusalem, the new eternal Jerusalem, what the writer of the book of Hebrews says Abraham was actually looking for (Heb. 11:10), the city with foundations whose architect and builder is God!

Its dimensions are approximately the same as from the Nile to the Euphrates, the Garden of Eden (paradise) restored, heaven and earth being made one in Messiah (Eph. 1:10). Even Yeshua as a blazing torch replaces the *menorah* (lampstand) in the new Jerusalem.

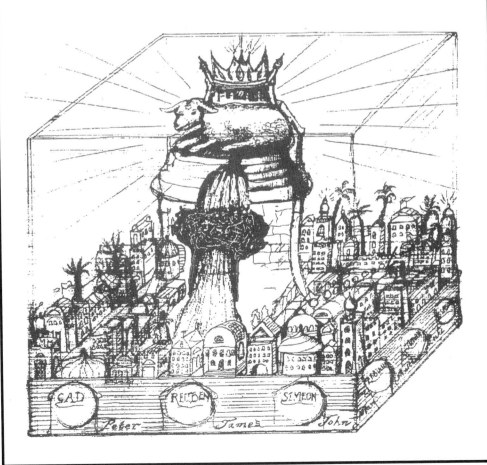

Revelation 21:1–22:5,12-14

"Then I saw a new heaven and a new earth, for the first heaven and the first earth had passed away, and there was no longer any sea. I saw the Holy City, the new Jerusalem, coming down out of heaven from God, prepared as a bride beautifully dressed for her husband. And I heard a loud voice from the throne saying, 'Now the dwelling of God is with men, and he will live with them. They will be his people, and God Himself will be with them and be their God. He will wipe away every tear from their eyes. There will be no more death or mourning or crying or pain, for the old order of things has passed away.'

"He who was seated on the throne said, 'I am making everything new!' Then he said, 'Write this down, for these words are trustworthy and true.' He said to me: 'It is done. I am the Alpha and the Omega, the Beginning and the End. To him who is thirsty I will give to drink without cost from the spring of the water of life. He who overcomes will inherit all this, and I will be his God and he will be my son. But the cowardly, the unbelieving, the vile, the murderers, the sexually immoral, those who practice magic arts, the idolaters and all liars—their place will be in the fiery lake of burning sulphur. This is the second death.'

"One of the seven angels who had the seven bowls full of the seven last plagues came and said to me, 'Come, I will show you the bride, the wife of the Lamb.' And he carried me away in the Spirit to a mountain great and high, and showed me the Holy City, Jerusalem, coming down out of heaven from God. It shone with the glory of God and its brilliance was like that of a very precious jewel, like a jasper, clear as crystal. It had a great, high wall with twelve gates, and with twelve angels at the gates. On the gates were written the names of the twelve tribes of Israel. There were three gates on the east, three on the north, three on the south and three on the west. The wall of the city had twelve foundations, and on them were the names of the twelve apostles of the Lamb. The angel who talked with me had a measuring rod of gold to measure the city, its gates and its walls. The city was laid out like a square, as long as it was wide. He measured the city with the rod and found it to be 12,000 stadia in length, and as wide and high as it is long. He measured its wall and it was 144 cubits thick, by man's measurement, which the angel was using. The wall was made of jasper, and the city of pure gold, as pure as glass. The foundations of the city walls were decorated with every kind of precious stone. The first foundation was jasper, the second sapphire, the third chalcedony, the fourth emerald, the fifth sardonyx, the sixth carnelian, the seventh chrysolite, the eighth beryl, the ninth topaz, the tenth chrysoprase, the eleventh jacinth, and the twelfth amethyst. The twelve gates were twelve pearls, each gate made of a single pearl. The great street of the city was of pure gold, like transparent glass. I did not see a temple in the city, because the Lord God Almighty and the Lamb are its temple. The city does not need the sun or the moon to shine on it, for the glory of God gives it light, and the Lamb is its lamp. The nations will walk by its light, and the kings of the earth will bring their splendor into it. On no day will its gates ever be shut, for there will be no night there. The glory and honor of the nations will be brought into it. Nothing impure will ever enter it, nor will anyone who does what is shameful or deceitful, but only those whose names are written in the Lamb's book of life.

"Then the angel showed me the river of the water of life, as clear as crystal, flowing from the throne of God and of the Lamb down the middle of the great street of the city. On each side of the river stood the tree of life, bearing twelve crops of fruit, yielding its fruit every month. And the leaves of the tree are for the healing of the nations. No longer will there be any curse. The throne of God and of the Lamb will be in the city, and his servants will serve him. They will see his face and his name will be on their foreheads. There will be no more night. They will not need the light of a lamp or the light of the sun, for the Lord God will give them light. And they will reign for ever and ever (Revelation 21:1–22:5).

"'Behold, I am coming soon! My reward is with me, and I will give to everyone according to what he has done. I am the Alpha and the Omega, the First and the Last, the Beginning and the End. Blessed are those who wash their robes, that they may have the right to the tree of life and may go through the gates into the city'" (Revelation 22:12-14).

John writes to the Church in Ephesus and says:

"He who has an ear let him hear what the Spirit says to the church. To Him who overcomes, I will give the right to eat from the tree of life, which is in the paradise of God" (Revelation 2:7).

John is writing to the church in Philadelphia saying he will make even angels come down from heaven at your feet and acknowledge that Yeshua loves you (Rev. 3:9).

"I am coming soon. Hold on to what you have, so that no one will take your crown. Him who overcomes I will make a pillar in the temple of my God. Never again will he leave it. I will write on him the name of my God and the name of the city of my God, the new Jerusalem, which is coming down out of heaven from my God; and I will also write on him my new name. He who has an ear, let him hear what the Spirit says to the churches" (Revelation 3:11-13).

May our lives and our prayers be for the peace of Jerusalem. He who loves her will prosper eternally and be secure in her King forever as a part of the new Jerusalem.

JERUSALEM WATCH OF THE KING

Worshipers and intercessors from the nations are encouraged to adopt their gate of Jerusalem. If you wish to come to Jerusalem for a Watchmen's Week or Prophetic Prayer Pilgrimage, we can introduce you to your gate-keeper in Jerusalem. Please prayerfully consider joining and praying during the indicated times (Israel times) for your Gateway to Jerusalem. Use the following two maps to help you.

Also, we strongly encourage you to use the book, *Prepare the Way for the King of Glory*. It is the only in-depth "spiritual map" of Jerusalem and contains valuable information on the redemptive purposes for the 12 Gates of Jerusalem. It also contains models and testimonies of different watches in Jerusalem and in the 12 Gateways back to Jerusalem.

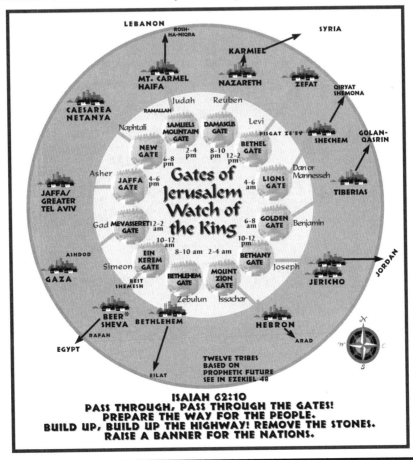

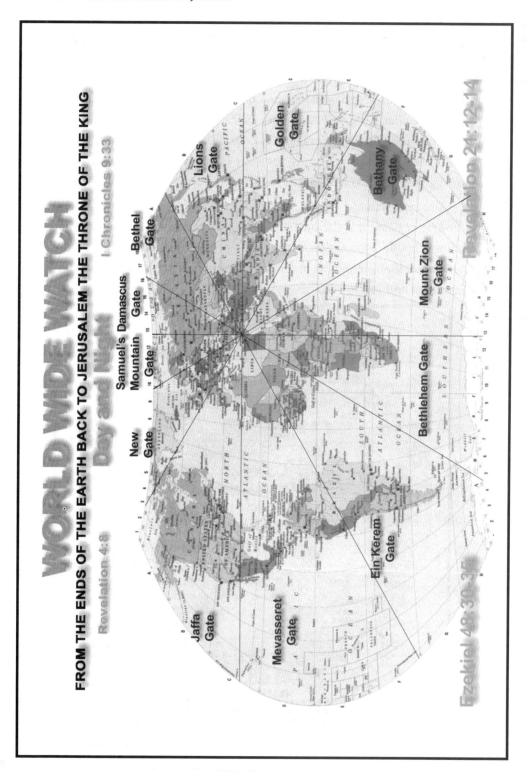

Scripture References

Chapter 1

Gen 31:51	Psa 122	Zech 12–14	Gal 4:26
II Sam 11:20	Isa 2:3	Matt 5:14	I Thess 5:3
II Chron 35:23	Isa 28:16	Matt 9:35-38	Heb 7:1-2
Job 38:6	Isa 42:6	Matt 23:37-39	Heb 12:22-24
Psa 14:7	Isa 55:8-9	John 1:14	

Chapter 2

Ex 33:19,20	Psa 46; 48	Isa 40:1-2; 62:1	Micah 6:8
Ex 34:5-7	Psa 50:1-2; 87	Ezek 43:6-7; 30-35	Amos 5:21-24
Song 5:10-16	Psa 132:14	Zech 13:12	Matt 9:36; 11:28
Josh 20:22	Psa 137	Zech 14:2-3	Luke 19:41-44
Psa 23:6	Isa 6; 62:4-7	Zech 20–21	I Cor 1:30
Psa 16:11; 45	Isa 9:6-7; 11:4	Zech 9:8-9	Rev 21:5

Chapter 3

Gen 22	Matt 5:33-35	John 8:56	Heb 11:8-10
Ex 3:16	Matt 23:37	Heb 7:3-4	Gal 4:24–5:1
Zech 13:1-2; 14:4	Luke 21:20-24, 29-30	Heb 9:12-15	

Chapter 4

Isa 62:1-2	Zech 12:6

Chapter 5

Gen 12:2-3,10	Gen 21:30-34	Isa 51:1-3	Luke 9:58
Gen 16:13-14	Isa 12:3	Heb11:8-10, 17-19	John 8.56,58

Chapter 6

Gen 2:9; 3:22; 13:10	Josh 24:15	Isa 19; 28:17-18	Rev 5:6; 11; 21:16
Gen 21:12-13	Psa 1:3	Zech 4	Rev 22:2
Gen 22:13-14	Psa 78	Rom 11	
	Isa 11:1-3; 42:6		

Chapter 7

Stone 1

Josh 5:13-14	Isa 9:6-7	Isa 62:10	Phil 1:21
Prov 28:1	Isa 40:3-5	Acts 3:21	Rev 6:10-12

Stone 2

Deut 6:4	Isa 11:15	Hos 11:1	Matt 2:15
Isa 9:6	Isa 19:23-25	Zech 12:10; 14:9	Col 12:15
	Isa 51:1-3		

Stone 3

Isa 2:6-10	Isa 49:22	Ezek 39:27-28	Heb 12:26
Isa 11:11-16	Isa 56:7	Hosea 11:10-11	Eph 6:12
Isa 14:1-2	Jer 1:10	Amos 9:14-15	
	Jer 16:14-16	Hag 2:2	

Stone 4

Isa 51:11	Jer 1:10	Micah 2:13	Luke 21
	Jer 30:1		

Stone 5

Isa 43:6	Ezek 37	Rom 11:15-19	Heb 12
	Micah 2:12-14	I Cor 15:44-46	

Stone 6

Ex 20:13	Psa 83:1-4

Stone 7

Isa 2:1-3	Ezek 43:7	Luke 21:29-31,34	Matt 24:14
Isa 56:7-8	Matt 21:13	Rom 11:25-27	Luke 21:32

Stone 8

Psa 14:7; 80	Isa 40:1	Zech 12:10–13:1	John 1:11
	Dan 9	Luke 19:41-44	Rom 1:16

Stone 9

Psa 32:8	Matt 26:6-13	Jas 4:4-5	Rev 19:9
Isa 62:2-4,7	Luke 12:22-40	Rev 1:14,16	Rev 1:7-8
	Phil 4:8		

Stone 10

Luke 21:28-33,36	Psa 122:6

Chapter 8

Zech 1:2	Zech 12–14	Zech 21:1-5	Rev 21:10-22

Chapter 9

Gen 15:18-19	Isa 11–19	Zech 12	Col 1:27
Lev 6:8-9,12-13	Ezek 38:8,11	Mal 3:2-4	Heb 12
I Ki 18:24	Zech 2:4-5	Mal 4	Rev 1:14-16

Watchmen's Materials

House of Prayer for All Nations

A collection of 200 nations' redemptive purposes, key 24-hour Watches and other useful information, *House of Prayer for All Nations* is a watchman's arsenal to help watchmen proclaim, pray and praise their way through the nations of the earth.

ISBN: 965-7193-09-5 $14

God's Abrahamic Covenants with Israel & the Church

This book is a biblical road map towards reconciliation that gives prophetic clarity from the Word of God on how God's covenants with the land of Israel, the Jewish people and the Church are for today and forever.

ISBN: 965-7193-13-3 $14

Sons of Abraham

Testimonies of Jewish and Arab leaders throughout the last two centuries, prophetic acts and convocations in the last 20 years, and a synopsis of the restoration of the Church in Egypt, Israel and Assyria, in this book show how God is preparing the way for fullness.

ISBN: 965-7193-03-6 $14

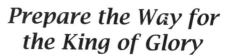

Prepare the Way for the King of Glory

An in-depth manual for the spiritual map of Jerusalem designed to equip watchmen for their task of praying for Jerusalem and Israel.

ISBN: 965-7193-02-8 $14

Let My People Go!

In the return of the Jews to Israel, Tom Hess sees the prophetically promised turning point in history. This book is an impassioned appeal to Jewry worldwide to resume their God-given role as "a light to the nations."

ISBN: 965-7193-12-5 $ 10

The Watchmen

In this book, Tom Hess will help you to assume your role as a watchman.

ISBN: 965-7193-00-1 $14

Transforming Your World

Author John Mulinde shares on breaking the yokes of your world from the individual to national level and coming to a higher place of glory in God where the Kingdom of God thrives.

ISBN: 965-7193-19-2 $14

JOIN US FOR THE ANNUAL

ALL NATIONS CONVOCATION JERUSALEM
WORLD WIDE WATCH CONVOCATION

AND

WATCHMEN'S TOUR OF ISRAEL

HIGHLIGHTS INCLUDE

Ten days and nights in Jerusalem.

Focused intercession, worship and teaching from some of the great prophetic and apostolic leaders of this age.

Touring Jerusalem with on-site intercession on the 12 Gates of Jerusalem.

Celebrating Rosh Hashana and Yom Kippur with the local body of Jewish and Arab believers from Jerusalem, Israel and all the Middle East.

Three days and nights touring the Holy Land guided by professionals to stand with local ministries in prayer, intercede at key locations like the four altars, and worship in the same places Yeshua did.

For more information about specific dates and costs or to request a registration form, please contact us:

www.jhopfan.org
ancj@jhopfan.org
+972-2-626-1518 / 627-4126
TOLL FREE from the US 1-888-513-9580
Fax +972-2-626-4239

TOM HESS

Called to stand with God for His purposes for Jerusalem, Tom Hess has lived on the peak of the Mount of Olives since 1987 at the Golden Gate House of Prayer with the most direct view possible of the Golden Gate and the Temple Mount. He is the Pastor of the Jerusalem House of Prayer for All Nations and Pastoral Gatekeeper of the Golden Gate and the Bethany–Bethphage Gate, contributing to both the 24-hour Watch at the Jerusalem House of Prayer for All Nations, the Jerusalem Watch of the King and the World Wide Watch. He is the president of the All Nations Convocation Jerusalem and Progressive Vision Publishing.

Tom Hess is the author of numerous books presenting an authentic view of issues surrounding Israel, Jerusalem and the Middle East. In his books you will enjoy such topics as God's covenants with the people and land of Israel, reconciliation of Jews and Arabs, *aliyah* and prayer. Tom also travels the world sharing God's heart for the covenant land and the covenant people while encouraging new 24-hour Watches to be birthed.

PROGRESSIVE VISION PUBLISHING

How beautiful upon the mountains are the feet of him that brings good tidings, that publishes peace; that brings good tidings of good, that publishes salvation; that says unto Zion, Thy God reigns! Isaiah 52:7